# ECONOMIC GROWTH IN THE THIRD WORLD

A Publication of the Economic Growth Center, Yale University

# ECONOMIC GROWTH IN THE THIRD WORLD: AN INTRODUCTION

## LLOYD G. REYNOLDS

Yale University Press     New Haven and London

The chapters in this book have been previously published in
Lloyd G. Reynolds, *Economic Growth in the Third World, 1850–1980,*
A Publication of the Economic Growth Center, Yale University (New
Haven: Yale University Press, 1985).

Designed by James J. Johnson
and set in Times Roman type by the Composing Room of Michigan.
Printed in the United States of America by
Vail-Ballou Press, Binghamton, New York.

*Library of Congress Cataloging-in-Publication Data*

Reynolds. Lloyd George, 1910–
    Economic growth in the Third World.

    (Publication of the Economic Growth Center, Yale
University)
    Bibliography: p.
    Includes index.
    1. Developing countries—Economic conditions.
2. Economic history—1945–     . I. Title. II. Series.
HC59.7.R476   1986        338.9′009172′4        85–20263
ISBN 0–300–03651–5 (alk. paper)
        0–300–03678–7 (paper)

The paper in this book meets the guidelines for permanence
and durability of the Committee on Production Guidelines
for Book Longevity of the Council on Library Resources.

10   9   8   7   6   5   4   3   2   1

# Contents

# Tables

# Foreword

This volume is one in a series of studies supported by the Economic Growth Center, a research organization within the Yale Department of Economics. The Center was created in 1961 to analyze, both theoretically and empirically, the process of economic growth and the economic relations between the developing and economically advanced countries. The research program emphasizes the search for regularities in the process of growth and changes in economic structure by means of cross-sectional and intertemporal studies and the analysis of policies that affect that process. An increasing share of the research involves statistical study of the behavior of households and firms as revealed in sample surveys by means of the application of microeconomic theory. Current projects include research on technology choice and transfer, household consumption, investment and demographic behavior, agricultural research and productivity growth, commodity market stabilization, labor markets and the returns to education and migration, income distribution, and international economic relations, including monetary and trade policies. The Center's research facility hold appointments in the Department of Economics and accordingly have teaching as well as research responsibilities.

The Center administers, jointly with the Department of Economics, the Yale master's degree program in International and Development Economics, in which most students have experiences as economists in foreign central banks, finance ministries, and public and private development agencies. It presents a regular series of workshops on development and trade and on microeconomics of labor and population and includes among its publications book-length studies, such as this, reprints by staff members, and discussion papers.

T. PAUL SCHULTZ, *Director*

# Preface

Courses in American and European economic history are a standard feature of the economics curriculum. Before 1945 other parts of the world were relatively neglected. But since then there has been a multiplication of courses on major countries (Japan, China, India), or on particular regions (Latin America, Southeast Asia), or even on third-world economies as a whole.

There is now a large research literature to provide underpinnings for such courses. In a systematic canvass of monographs on third-world economies, extending over several years, I was rather surprised to find more than four hundred books that deserved careful reading. But the very abundance of the literature makes it difficult to get an overview of third-world economic growth as a whole. To provide such an overview is the main purpose of this book.

When I call it an "introduction," I mean precisely that. It is in no way a substitute for careful reading of country experience. But I hope that these chapters, and the attached bibliography, will be helpful in leading students farther into the subject.

This book is a companion volume to—indeed, is wholly derived from—my larger study *Economic Growth in the Third World, 1850–1980*. That book, which includes brief historical sketches of the larger third-world economies, grew eventually to a length that placed it beyond most students' patience and pocketbooks. Thus it seemed useful to take the generalizing chapters from the larger book and make them available in a more convenient format. Students interested in a particular country will find the relevant section of *Economic Growth* useful as a lead-in, though it can be no more than that.

Some of the ideas in chapters 1–4 have been published in different form in "The Spread of Economic Growth to the Third World, 1850–1980," *Journal of Economic Literature,* XXI (September)1983, pp. 941–81. I am grateful to the American Economic Association for permission to reprint portions of pages 959–64 in that article.

I am grateful also to the Mellon Foundation for financing what must have seemed at the outset a high-risk enterprise. A number of colleagues have provided helpful criticism at various stages of the work. Janet Armitage and Adrienne Cheasty bore the brunt of the bibliographical and statistical work, and Roberta Milano-Ottenbreit handled the manuscript with her usual care and efficiency. I owe a special debt to Dr. Mary T. Reynolds for a fine analytical index.

# ECONOMIC GROWTH IN THE THIRD WORLD

# 1

## The Study of Long-Term Growth

Until recently economic history meant the economic history of Western Europe and the United States. This was what we were taught in graduate school and what we dutifully retaught our students. Other parts of the world were outside the mainstream—they were the province of orientalists, Africanists, and other regional specialists, whose work was little regarded by economists.

After 1945 this situation began to change, essentially for political reasons. During the next twenty years the number of independent countries multiplied remarkably, as one colony after another became self-governing. Quite soon the new countries decisively outnumbered the old. The United Nations and its specialized agencies provided a forum in which new countries could voice their complaints and their needs. With the growing political-military rivalry between the North Atlantic Treaty Organization and the Soviet blocs, nonaligned nations tended to be regarded as potential allies or enemies, and competition for their allegiance became a major diplomatic sport. The "foreign-aid boom" may have owed a little to humanitarian sentiment, and even a little to economic analysis, but it owed much more to international politics.

Social scientists, like judges, follow the election returns; and these strong political tides soon rippled over into the world of scholarship. There was a rapid multiplication, especially in the United States, of research centers, foundation and government grants, specialists and courses in economic development, and advisory missions to foreign countries. The research literature on non-Western economies grew from a trickle in the late 1940s to a flood by the 1960s.

This literature focused heavily on recent events and current problems. Much of it, indeed, was devoted to researching the future in that it explored policies and programs for future growth. A conventional wisdom of economic development grew up rather rapidly. Third-world countries were viewed as lined up, more or less equally, at the threshold of economic growth. They had a future, but no past. Third-world countries were structurally different from the "more-developed countries" and would have to develop along different lines. Old rules of the game no longer applied. In particular, foreign trade could no longer be relied on as an engine of growth because of the bleak outlook for primary exports. Development policies must emphasize reduction of imports and greater self-sufficiency.

In fact, little was known about the economic structure or past growth record of most third-world countries. As Ian Little comments, "A priori postulation and premature stereotyping ran far ahead of empirical research. Hypotheses were accepted as facts, and it has taken years of patient work to undermine the myths thus created. . . . Subsequent research and events have shown that most of the presumptions . . . were wrong."*

Beginning around 1960, the intellectual climate began to change. "Neo-classical economics," previously ignored or explicitly rejected, was rehabilitated and applied to empirical problems. An increasing flow of research revealed, not surprisingly, that economic behavior in third-world economies had much in common with economic behavior elsewhere. Alongside those who were researching the future, some economists turned to researching the past. A growing number of solid monographs on particular countries, often going back to 1900 or beyond, appeared.

This country-specific literature has now accumulated to impressive proportions. The bibliography at the end of this volume, which includes only material available in English, runs to more than four hundred books. There is plenty of reading material to support courses on the economic history of particular regions or of the third world as a whole; and such courses are appearing in increasing numbers, as options or supplements to the standard European and American courses. But no one to my knowledge has undertaken to review and digest the country material and to fit it into a systematic framework. This is the main object of the present study. The discussion may also serve as a corrective to some earlier misconceptions. As against the view that "life began in 1950," I hope to show that the third world has a rich record of prior growth, beginning for most countries in the 1850–1914 era. I hope also to show that growth patterns in third-world countries bear some resemblance to those observed earlier in Europe and North America.

An immersion in the country literature inevitably tempts one to generalize. What does it all add up to? How and why does a country's per capita income, previously stationary, embark on a sustained uptrend? Can economic growth, once initiated, be counted on to continue indefinitely? As per capita income continues to rise, is there a standard pattern of change in the composition and distribution of output? Have growth patterns since World War II differed significantly from those observed before World War II?

These are large questions, which no one study can hope to resolve. But the temptation to suggest answers is there, and I have not resisted it entirely. In later chapters I shall occasionally suggest generalizations, which for brevity must be stated in a way that may appear dogmatic. The reader should understand that these

*Ian M. D. Little, *Economic Development* (New York: Basic Books, 1982), pp. 118–19.

generalizations are less firm in my own mind than they may appear on paper. Further, there are hardly any general statements to which one cannot find exceptions in one country or another. I shall look at such exceptions and try to do justice to the rich variety of country experience.

SCOPE OF THE STUDY

The countries with which I am concerned go by a variety of names. *Underdeveloped* was abandoned rather early as carrying a stigma. *Less developed* is still commonly used. But less developed than what? By what tests, or in what dimensions? The United Nations and other political bodies tend to use the more complimentary term *developing,* but it unfortunately does not describe all countries in the group. *Third world* is a political term, meant to designate countries that are neither part of the OECD (Organization for Economic Cooperation and Development) or of the Soviet–East European bloc. Although I shall use it here for brevity, it has little economic meaning. The countries included under this rubrik, which comprise most of the world's surface and population, differ widely in size, resource base, income level, growth rate, and economic structure.

It is best to admit frankly that the definition of our universe is geographic. It embraces the continents of Asia, Africa, and Central and South America, excluding only Vietnam and North Korea because of poor documentation and South Africa because of its relatively high income level and special socioeconomic characteristics. The late-developing countries of southern and eastern Europe are analogous in some ways to those considered here, but to include them would have stretched an already large undertaking to unmanageable proportions.

Even the three continents I am considering are unmanageable in the sense of including 120 independent countries. To simplify the task, I have generally excluded countries with a population in 1980 of less than ten million. (I have cheated slightly in order to secure a reasonable representation of African countries. Ivory Coast, Zambia, and Zimbabwe, which are included, are somewhat below the ten million mark.) This tactic gets rid of some 80 countries at one stroke, reducing the sample to 41. The exclusion is unfortunate in that small economies have special characteristics, notably heavier dependence on foreign trade. But it does not appear to bias the sample with respect to economic success. Comparative analysis of country growth rates over the period 1950–80 shows no significant relation between growth rate and country size. The spectacular performance of Singapore and Hong Kong is offset by miserable performance in some other small economies.

The countries included, then, are as follows:

| | |
|---|---|
| *Latin America* | Argentina, Brazil, Chile, Colombia, Cuba, Mexico, Peru, Venezuela |
| *North Africa and Middle East* | Algeria, Egypt, Iran, Iraq, Morocco, Sudan, Turkey |

*Africa (sub-Saharan)*          Ethiopia, Ghana, Ivory Coast, Kenya,
                                Mozambique, Nigeria, Tanzania, Uganda,
                                Zaire, Zambia, Zimbabwe
*Asia*                          Afghanistan, Bangladesh, Burma, China,
                                India, Indonesia, Japan, Malaysia, Nepal,
                                Pakistan, Philippines, South Korea, Sri
                                Lanka, Taiwan, Thailand

Present-day country names have been employed here; in some cases they differ from names used during the colonial period. Problems of boundary change on the Indian subcontinent have been taken into account. Taiwan is a province of China rather than a country but has followed a separate development path for almost a century, which seems worth reporting. Some might question the inclusion of Japan, whose high and sustained growth rate has led it to be classified since 1950 among the advanced industrial countries. But Japan's economic success should not rule it out of consideration with the 1880–1940 era, any more than the remarkable success of Taiwan and South Korea should rule them out for the 1950– 80 period.

In addition to limiting country coverage, some restriction of scope was necessary to hold the study within manageable bounds. The main focus is on economic growth, in the simplest Kuznetsian sense of an increase in capacity to produce. But this restriction is not as serious as it might appear. Almost everything that happens in an economy will affect its growth rate. So the question of how economic growth begins and how it proceeds over the course of time will lead into areas as diverse as agricultural productivity, the typical sequence of industrialization, patterns of foreign trade, sources and uses of public revenue, and the ways in which growth can be stimulated or retarded by government action.

The emphasis on growth is not meant to downgrade such other important dimensions of national economic performance as institutional improvement, the level of employment, and the distribution of income. Indeed, a good deal will be said about these things. Reliable data on income distribution, however, are limited to recent decades and to a few countries and are still too fragile to support sweeping generalizations.

A further restriction, evident from the bibliography, is that I have relied mainly on writings by economists and economic historians, with only sporadic forays into related social science disciplines. This no doubt imparts a certain bias to the discussion. I have tended to follow the economists' habit of assuming that economies everywhere behave more or less similarly and that, if they are sufficiently insulated from political shock and other exogenous disasters, they will go about the business of development and growth. In this view third-world countries are much like those of the first world and will, with a modicum of external aid and internal stability, follow in the path of their predecessors.

Although there is an element of truth in this view, it is also in some ways limited. One perceptive reviewer of this manuscript commented that most third-world societies do not have the value systems required to generate economic development from within; and also that I had not taken adequate account of political variables. He remarked that

> some of these countries (Argentina is an example) have seen their promise blighted by internecine conflict. They have been, as it were, derailed; and with luck, may yet get back on the rails. But this raises the question whether political stability is not also related to internal characteristics. . . . [The author] could do much more to stress the degree to which appropriate and effective forms of government are a function not only of experience, but also—and once again—of values. I am thinking here of such things as the shift from office as property (an opportunity for personal enrichment) to office as function (a bundle of tasks and obligations). Or of the shift from personal power to the rule of law.

I have much sympathy with these comments. But one person can do only so much; and the ideal volume would never have been finished. In the two concluding chapters I have tried, in a very amateur way, to assess the impact of political variables on a country's growth performance. But the study is no doubt still too "economic" in tone. Perhaps in time someone with broader social science skills will be able to put more flesh on this bare-bones narrative.

### THE CONCEPTION OF GROWTH

Studies of national economic growth tend to begin with the point at which one observes a sustained rise in per capita income and to focus on experience after that point. But what is going on "before the curtain rises"? Rarely, if ever, does the rise in per capita income begin from a situation of stationary population size and national output. Anything resembling the "classical stationary state" would be hard to find in modern times. Rather, one observes in most countries during the eighteenth and early nineteenth centuries that population is growing slowly and national ouput is rising at about the same rate. A situation in which population and output are growing at roughly the same rate, with no secular rise of per capita output, I define as *extensive growth*.

Kuznets's view is that this is genuine growth, deserving of study. A similar view is taken in an interesting study by Ashok Guha (1981), who regards growth as biological adaptation to environment. A species that is able to reproduce itself and increase in numbers is a successful species.

I share this view for several reasons. Empirically, the era in which population and output are growing without a rise in per capita output is usually quite long (in China, it is said to have lasted for some six centuries before 1949). To omit this period, then, is to omit a substantial part of the growth story. Analytically, the conventional procedure in which the rate of population growth is simply deducted from the rate of gross domestic product (GDP) growth to arrive at what is *defined* as "economic growth" reduces population growth to secondary importance. A broader definition, under which economic growth begins when population growth begins, has the merit of restoring population analysis to a more prominent place. Finally, some developments that arise during an era of extensive growth, if not strictly prerequisite to a later rise in per capita output, are at least helpful in facilitating it. There is considerable continuity in the evolution of an economy.

Of the 41 countries in our sample, seven seem still to be in the extensive-growth era. But in the remaining countries, at various points in time between 1850 and 1965, the beginnings of a sustained rise in per capita output can be observed— sustained in the sense that, although year-to-year growth rates are uneven, per capita output does not fall back to its initial level. I call the point at which this happens the *turning point*. In chapter 3 I shall date the turning point for each country, but it should be understood that there is nothing magical about this date. Rather, I mean to draw attention to a period of a decade or so before and after the date. The turning point can be identified only in retrospect; it will usually be a decade or more before a trend is certain rather than a temporary upswing to be followed by relapse.

I call the sustained rise in per capita output after the turning point *intensive growth*. This does not mean that the future beyond the turning point is entirely predictable. There is predictability in the sense that, so long as per capita output continues to rise, there will be systematic changes in the composition and uses of national output, the broad contours of which have been charted by Kuznets, Chenery, and others. But the growth rate of per capita output will fluctuate in response to swings in the world economy, harvest variations, resource discoveries, and other circumstances. In addition to such fluctuations, there are countries—Japan, Taiwan, Korea—in which the trend rate of growth has accelerated over the long run. There is one notable case, Argentina, in which growth has decelerated gradually over the past century. There are also cases, such as Ghana, Uganda, and Zambia, in which growth has changed to stagnation or decline. The turning point is not an insurance policy for all future time.

My schema thus includes three chronological stages: an era of extensive growth, followed (in cases of success) by a turning point, followed by an era of intensive growth extending in most cases to the present day. I find this schema useful in organizing historical experience and will follow it in later chapters. But it also invites misunderstanding, because the same terms have been used with different meanings by other economists. So some further distinctions are in order.

Readers of the literature on agriculture will recall the distinction between the *extensive margin of cultivation,* on which previously unused land is being brought into production, and the *intensive margin of cultivation,* on which more labor and other variable inputs are being applied to previously cultivated acres. Here *extensive* and *intensive* are clearly being used in a quite different sense. The extensive and intensive margins do not form a chronological sequence. They coexist at each point in time and are extended in a balanced way that equates marginal productivity of the variable factors on the two margins.

There is still some danger of confusion, because expansion of acreage on the extensive margin of cultivation is usually a prominent feature of my era of extensive growth. Eventually, as population continues to grow, all cultivable land is occupied and the extensive margin vanishes. Continued increases in agricultural output are then dependent on application of more variable inputs at the intensive margin, accompanied by innovation in crops and production methods. It is quite possible, even usual, for efforts in these directions to succeed in raising food output in line with population growth. We may thus see a continuation of *extensive growth* (in my sense) accomplished by continuing effort on the *intensive margin* of cultivation.

Thus there is no necessary correspondence in time between the end of the frontier and the end of my extensive-growth era. There are cases—Egypt, for example—in which land was fully occupied long *before* the turning point. But there are many more cases in which the end of the frontier came well *after* the turning point. Indeed, a surprising number of third-world countries still have reserves of unused land.

A word now about turning points. My turning point marks the transition from a stationary to a rising trend of per capita output, a transition that is arguably important. But after my turning point, that is, within the intensive-growth era, there are additional dates that have sometimes been regarded as turning points and that are also important. One of these is the point at which declining birthrates overtake declining deathrates, so that the rate of natural increase begins to fall. This point, which in northwestern Europe and North America was passed before 1900, has been passed by some third-world countries only since 1960, and in most of those countries it still lies in the future. Another significant date is that at which the agricultural labor force, which goes on increasing for a long time after our turning point, finally begins to shrink in absolute size. This marks a late stage of intensive growth, a stage at which the suction of labor demand into urban activities is strong enough to absorb more than the natural increase of population in rural areas.

Perhaps most significant is the Lewis (1954) turning point, which appears also in the Fei-Ranis (1964) model as the "commercialization point," at which an assumed initial pool of surplus labor has been drained dry and the real wage level begins to rise. I shall have more to say about this concept in chapter 4. The relevant point here is that this is also a late stage of the growth story. In Japan, for example, I date the turning point at 1880, but the Lewis turning point was reached only in the 1920s. I date the turning point for Taiwan in 1895, and for Korea in 1910, the dates of Japanese colonization; but Taiwan and South Korea reached the Lewis turning point only in the late 1960s. For China, my turning point is 1949, but the Lewis turning point has not yet been reached.

Walt Rostow's "takeoff" concept (1956) has not fared well in the literature, but a word should be added about it. Rostow tends to identify growth with industrialization and to date a country's takeoff as the point at which one sees a substantial development of factory industry. In my schema, the turning point is typically characterized by an acceleration of agricultural (or occasionally mineral) output and a rising foreign-trade ratio. Rising income from exports does broaden the domestic market for manufactures, but the initial supply response comes mainly from handicraft workshops and small-scale industries. There is usually a lag of several decades before factory industry becomes prominent, though this lag has been shorter since 1950 than it was in earlier times.

Thus Rostow's takeoff datings (1978) are typically too late, sometimes much too late, from my point of view. A few examples may be useful:

| Country | Reynolds Turning Point | Rostow Takeoff |
|---|---|---|
| Argentina | 1860 | 1933–50 |
| Brazil | 1880 | 1933–50 |
| Mexico | 1873 | 1940–60 |
| South Korea | 1910 | 1961–68 |
| Taiwan | 1895 | 1953–60 |
| Thailand | 1850 | 1960–70 |

Further, Rostow posited a "takeoff into self-sustained growth." This implies that, once the plane is off the ground, it moves up smoothly to a stable cruising altitude. My turning point carries no such guarantee. Some countries in my sample have managed to do less well in recent decades than they were doing at an earlier time, and in some cases per capita output fell during the 1970s.

My turning-point dates are early, most of them falling between 1850 and 1914. This will raise at least two questions in readers' minds. First, until recently most of these areas were colonies rather than independent countries. In 17 cases my turning point falls within the colonial era. Can a country really develop in a significant sense under colonial rule? Second, in almost every case the turning point is associated with a sharp rise in exports of agricultural or mineral products. Much of the recent development literature is critical of growth led by primary exports. Such a growth pattern is sometimes regarded as "colonial" or "neo-colonial," benefiting the industrial countries rather than the primary-product suppliers, and even as unviable over the long run. These questions deserve more attention than is feasible in an introductory chapter and will be considered at some length in chapter 3.

THE METHOD OF ANALYSIS

Having defined economic growth, I now must consider how to set about analyzing it. In my view, countries are the basic unit of study, and national time series are the main raw material.

Economic growth occurs within units of varying size: farms and business enterprises, cities, regions, countries. But among these, the nation is most significant. *Nation* is used here to include colonies, a view I shall try to justify in chapter 3. Some degree of political unification, of continuity in government, of external peace and internal order seems necessary before growth can begin. Further, economic interaction is more intense within national boundaries than across them. And a nation can in principle control economic events within its borders but not beyond them. Thus efforts to understand long-term growth must start from the experience of individual countries. National case studies are the building blocks for growth analysis.

This view, however, is open to challenge from two directions. Some would urge regional units as at least equally important. In large countries such as India, China, or Brazil there are well-known differences in regional income levels and growth rates, and the significance of national averages may well be questioned. Indeed, regional income differences probably tend to widen during the early decades of intensive growth. But over the longer run they tend to narrow again; and they narrow precisely because the regions are part of a nation, making possible relatively free movement of factors and the application of national economic policies to reduce inequality. The disequalizing effects of growth, emphasized by Myrdal and others, do not seem to dominate over the long run.

An opposite and perhaps more trenchant criticism is that analysis should focus on the world economy and that it is the position of a country within this larger structure that determines its economic fate. Several strands of thought recur in this literature: the argument that most third-world countries were long exploited by the colonial powers and that many are still exploited under a system of "neo-colonialism"; the "dependencia" or "unequal exchange" view that third-world nations are inherently disadvantaged in the world trading system; the view, advanced most recently by Immanuel Wallerstein (1979), that the core-periphery distinction is fundamental and that the exploited peripheral countries are essential to the functioning of the core countries. It follows that all countries cannot develop simultaneously.

A critical review of this literature would require a separate essay. On the whole, I find it unconvincing. Much of it appears doctrinaire and nonempirical, more concerned with reasoning from general principles than with careful observation of reality. It flies in the face of the evidence of massive economic progress in many countries since 1945.

Even if one finds the core-periphery schema useful, one must admit that nations do not remain locked in position within this schema. Japan would certainly have been classified as peripheral in 1880. Today, it is part of the core. Quite a few other middle-income countries have achieved at least "semi-core" status. The world economy offers opportunities as well as constraints, but nations differ in their ability to take advantage of these opportunities. The world economic boom of 1850–1914, and the more recent boom of 1945–73, offered increased opportunities to move from extensive to intensive growth. Yet in each of these periods, some countries were able to climb onto the growth escalator while others were not. What makes the difference? Generalized complaints about exploitation of third world countries do not provide a satisfactory answer.

In reviewing historical experience, I have been impressed with the degree of *mobility* among national economies. Countries are continuously reranking themselves in the national-income league, through widely differing rates of progress. This is at least as true of third-world countries as of the "developed" countries, where there has also been considerable reranking since 1945. The interesting question is why the growth rate of per capita income should differ so widely among countries. It would seem that efforts at explanation should focus not on the world economic environment, which to some extent is common to all, but on the internal dynamics of each national economy.

Having chosen countries as the unit, and having compiled a list of 41, I turn next to the question, What would we like to know about them? The ideal data bank would consist of long time series for each country, measuring a rather obvious list of economic magnitudes, beginning at some point in the period of extensive growth and continuing through the turning point to the present day. What we actually have falls far short of this ideal. For the long period before 1940, the data are quite fragmentary. They relate mainly to things which governments tend to measure for administrative purposes, including the following.

1. *Population.* For most parts of the world other than tropical Africa there are estimates of population size going back for several centuries. Dana Durand (1974) has reviewed these estimates and has assigned quality grades, A through D, to countries and major regions. The ratings for 1750 are quite poor, with many areas receiving C and D grades and only Japan getting an A. By 1900, however, the ratings are much better, with no D grades and only three Cs. This improvement over time would no doubt hold true also for trade statistics and other economic data, though I have not found any Durand-type ratings. This qualitative change in time-series data obviously increases the difficulty of drawing conclusions from them. What appears to be an increase in quantity may partly reflect more complete enumeration.

2. *Foreign Trade.* Foreign trade is measured in the course of applying export and import duties, a major source of government revenue in earlier times. In addition to value totals, which raise serious problems of deflation, there are often physical series for principal export and import products. The data are somewhat impaired by smuggling activities, but the fact that trade flows are recorded by both participating countries permits cross-checking for accuracy. The primary data on trade have been worked over quite thoroughly by Kuznets (1967), Lewis (1969), Maizels (1968), and others, and economic historians have usually exploited the data available for their countries.

3. *Government Finance.* Again, accuracy of reporting varies with the political structure and with honesty and competence in public administration. The best

accounts are usually for colonial areas where the metropolitan government, concerned that the colony should be self-supporting, required a detailed accounting of revenues and expenditures.

4. *Agricultural Acreage and Output*. This area is not very well documented. Instead of the continuous time series we would like to have, there are fragments of information for scattered years and on a variety of subjects. They include: total cultivated acreage; percent of acreage that is irrigated; acreage devoted to each major crop—interesting because there is often considerable change in the composition of output even during the period of extensive growth; occasionally, estimates of yields per acre for particular crops. Information on yields is sparse, however, and historians tend to assume constant yields in the absence of a better alternative and in the absence of significant evidence of technical progress.

Information on national output, then, reduces to output of export products, government output, and limited information on domestic food production. Manufacturing production, which at this stage is carried on mainly in households and handicraft workshops, is essentially unmeasured; so too is trade and production of private services. Thus the conclusions one finds in economic histories of individual countries are almost invariably qualitative, taking the form "there is no indication of an increase in per capita output *before* such-and-such date" or "per capita income seems to have been rising appreciably *after* such-and-such date." Here the historian is trying to judge what the time series of total and per capita output would look like if they were actually available. And I, standing on the shoulders of the country specialists, can only report these judgments without trying to improve them.

For the years since 1945 the situation is better. The United Nations and its specialized agencies, as well as the International Bank for Reconstruction and Development (IBRD), International Monetary Fund (IMF), OECD, and other organizations, regularly collect national accounts and a great variety of other economic measurements from almost every country. The quality of the national accounts, to be sure, still varies widely from country to country. But imperfect numbers, interpreted with due caution, are better than no numbers at all. I shall mine this data bank at some length in a later chapter.

Frustration at the scarcity of really long time series has led to widespread resort to cross-section studies as a partial substitute. In the 1950s, indeed, this was the only possible course. Countries were arranged in order of per capita income in U.S. dollars as of a particular year, and per capita income was then used as an independent variable to explore differences in economic structure.

Such studies are interesting and important in their own right. They have confirmed many systematic differences in the structure of production and employment for countries at differing income levels. In general, recent work by Chenery and others supports the earlier findings of Clark, Hoffman, and Kuznets.

It is wrong, however, to regard cross-section analyses as a satisfactory substitute for longitudinal studies. The reasons are partly technical and statistical—

distortions in the conversion of national currencies to U.S. dollar equivalents, differences in regression coefficients derived from cross-section as against time-series data, and so on. But the matter goes deeper than this. Cross-section analysis at a single point in time cannot reproduce the richness of events over time. It cannot answer such key questions as why a particular country reaches a turning point at one time rather than another or why, during a particular time period, some countries grow considerably faster than others. Nor can it illuminate the qualitative changes in economic and political institutions that typically accompany growth and that may either accelerate or impede it. Each country is a historically unique individual whose growth experience will not be replicated precisely by any other country. This sense of identity is lost when Ghana becomes simply $X_{33}$ in a supposedly homogeneous universe.

There is no satisfactory substitute for comparative analysis of national time series. This is the method pioneered by Kuznets in his classic studies of long-term growth in the "developed" countries. We can try to work in the spirit of Kuznets, even though the data do not allow us to replicate the precision of his results.

# 2

## The Era of Extensive Growth

The era in which population and output are growing at about the same rate is a long one. It typically lasts for a century or more, and in some countries extensive growth has been documented over several centuries. I propose to ask several questions about such a period:

1. How is the economy organized? What do we mean by such terms as *premodern, traditional,* or *subsistence economy?*
2. How and why does population begin to grow? How is food output increased to keep pace with population?
3. What changes do we observe in the organization of industry, trade, and other nonagricultural sectors? For example, does power-driven factory production ever appear before the turning point?
4. Finally, several analytical problems;
   a. When per capita income fails to rise, does this indicate the absence of significant change? Under these circumstances are we dealing with a "stationary state"?
   b. In classical economic models, population growth usually was associated with a change in per capita income—positive or negative, depending on the model. How can the economy increase in size without an appreciable change in per capita income?
   c. In what sense, if at all, can developments during the extensive-growth era be regarded as a preparation, or a precondition, for the later turning point to intensive growth?

ECONOMIC ORGANIZATION

What does the economy look like during a period of extensive growth? Some of the terms commonly used for this stage of development are not really very descriptive. We often speak of these economies as "traditional" or "conventional," the implication being that actions are guided by customary rules rather than economic calculation. In particular, the small peasant farmers who make up most of the population are portrayed as following traditional farming routines. This scenario surely overstates the role of custom and understates the importance of economic rationality. There is now abundant evidence that small peasant producers, in view of what they know and the constraints they face, behave just as economically as American farmers. In a situation where crop failure can mean disaster and even starvation, peasant farmers are sensibly averse to risk. But they are quite responsive to *demonstrated* opportunities for income improvement. As we shall see, introduction of new crops and methods for the intensification of cultivation is usually going on even during the extensive-growth period. And the later transition to intensive growth is heavily dependent on a "normal" farmer response to income incentives.

Another familiar term is *subsistence economy*. This has a dual connotation: people consume what they produce, and they live in some sense at a minimum or conventional level of "subsistence." Both statements contain an element of truth, but both are also treacherous. The ratio of home production to home consumption rarely approaches 100 percent, and it is certainly not invariant among countries or over time. The conventional level of "subsistence" is also flexible. In adverse periods, it can be depressed farther than one might have thought possible in advance. And it is quite flexible upward when conditions are improving.

It is better to say that the economy is dominated at the stage of extensive growth by *household production*. Each family produces not only most of its own food, but most of its housing and clothing, plus a wide range of services— education, healing, recreational activity, religious observance. We commonly observe that at this stage 80–90 percent of the population live in rural areas, on isolated farms or in small villages close to farmland. This was true in Europe in 1700, and the 80 percent ratio still holds in China today. This percentage is sometimes wrongly regarded as indicating the size of the agricultural sector. All it really means is that most economic activity is family activity. A careful record of time use by rural family members will reveal that agricultural activities take perhaps 50–60 percent of the total, the remainder going to "industrial" and service activities.

It follows that the apparent shrinkage of the agricultural sector and the swelling up of other sectors as economic growth proceeds is partly fictitious. In part, the shift represents a transfer of activities from households to specialized commercial producers, whose activities are more readily detected and measured. But people always have clothes and they always have housing, no matter how these goods are produced.

The prominence of household production is not inconsistent with a substantial amount of marketed output, a widespread development of markets, and trade and transport over long distances. Nor is it inconsistent with substantial changes in commodities, techniques, market organization, and trade routes over the course of time. What some might view as a "primitive" economy is in fact quite complex, sophisticated, and responsive to change.

In the case of Western European countries, this view would be readily accepted. It is well known that these economies became increasingly diversified, commercialized, and linked by trade relations during the sixteenth and seventeenth centuries. Well before the industrial era European economies experienced substantial development of towns and town markets, extensive development of manufacturing by handicraft methods, substantial interchange of goods between town and country, creeping technical progress in agriculture, internal trade along rivers and canals, and overseas trade around the shores of the Mediterranean and the Baltic and North seas.

There is a tendency, however, to assume that similar statements cannot be made about third-world countries, that their pre-turning point economies were less commercialized, more static, more agriculture-oriented than were their European counterparts. As evidence to the contrary, let us look briefly at three cases: China during the Ming and Ching dynasties; West Africa before 1900; and the contemporary Sherpa economy of northern Nepal.

## China

The case of China has been documented by Albert Feuerwerker (1968, 1969), Dwight Perkins (1969, 1975), Alexander Eckstein (1977), and others. The six centuries before 1949 can be regarded as an era of extensive growth, which had been going on more or less continuously since establishment of the Ming dynasty in 1368. Over this period the population of the country increased about eight times. What did the economy look like during these centuries?

Agriculture was central, but far from all-important. Feuerwerker estimates that agricultural output was about two-thirds of national output in the 1880s. This is close to Eckstein's estimate of 65 percent for 1933, suggesting the absence of significant structural change. The percentage of rural *population,* of course, was substantially higher—perhaps 80 percent of the total, as indeed it is today. But the rural population was doing many things besides growing foodstuffs.

Industry, which at this stage meant handicrafts, accounted for perhaps 7–8 percent of national output. This work was done mainly in individual farm households. But there was also cooperative activity by a number of households in rice milling, wheat milling, and salt and pottery production; and there were some larger workshops in urban areas. The trading activities, to be described later, constituted another 7–8 percent, and transport perhaps 5 percent, of national output. Government in the late nineteenth century was raising in taxes about 7.5 percent of national output, a figure not out of line with tax ratios in European countries during the nineteenth century.

The most notable feature of the centuries before 1900 was the gradual peopling of the country. The population in 1400 is estimated at 65–80 million, heavily concentrated in the lower Yangtze valley and along the east coast. From these areas people spread out to the south and southwest, west into the "rice bowl" of Szechwan, and north into the North China Plain. The process was still continuing in 1900 with expansion into Manchuria and Sinkiang, though land here was of lower quality than that settled earlier. The average growth rate of population before 1900 was about 0.4 percent by year, held to this level by occasional wars and famine as well as endemic diseases. The 1913 population is estimated at 430 ± 25 million.

If we assume, as China scholars generally do, that per capita food consumption changed little over this long period, then agricultural output must have risen roughly in line with population. How was this increase accomplished? The most obvious source is an increase in cultivated acreage, which grew about fourfold between 1400 and 1950. More interesting, however, is that yields per acre roughly doubled over this period, indicating that the "traditional economy" was not immune to technical change. Perkins (1969) notes several kinds of change:

1. Some improvement of seeds, partly developed and diffused within China, partly imported from abroad.
2. Introduction of new crops from America after 1600. Corn and potatoes were especially important, partly because they could be grown in areas not hospitable to other crops. As the frontier gradually closed and the man / land ratio rose after 1850, farmers adjusted to the decreasing availability of new land partly by shifting to crops (including cash crops such as cotton and raw silk) that yielded more food or income per acre and at the same time required more labor for their cultivation.
3. A gradual extension of double-cropping, accompanied by irrigation projects to provide the necessary control of water supply. By 1900 irrigation had been extended to almost all feasible acreage. Population growth in a sense *produced* more double-cropping by providing more labor both for seasonal peaks of cultivation and for water-control projects.
4. An increase of inputs, notably fertilizer inputs. More people produced more night soil! So did more pigs, whose numbers apparently kept up with population growth. Perkins suggests that, without this side benefit, pork production would have been unprofitable.

Trade was carried on in a stable hierarchy of markets, ranging from local to international in scope. Perhaps three-quarters of total trade went on in some 70,000 local markets, in which peasants and handicraftsmen exchanged their surplus produce. Local trade absorbed perhaps 20 percent of farm output, and this proportion seems not to have changed much over the centuries. Trade was thoroughly monetized and commercialized but restricted in geographic scope.

Longer-distance trade was restricted by transport costs and involved only objects of sufficient value to warrant the cost. Trade moved mainly along waterways, notably the vast Yangtze network, by vessels ranging from tiny sampans to large freighters. In northern China, less well supplied with waterways, most goods had to be moved by carts, which was slow and expensive. It is estimated that only 5–7 percent of national output went into interprovincial trade and perhaps 1–2 percent into foreign trade. Even by 1900 the trade network had changed only a little at the seacoast fringes and not at all within the country.

The government apparatus presiding over this economic activity was a meritocracy populated by the small educated elite. Perhaps because of the sheer size of the country, provincial and local governments were relatively more important than in smaller countries. Regular (or irregular) tribute was paid to the Emperor, but the Emperor was far away. Scholars estimate that even in the 1890s only 40 percent of tax revenues went to the central government. Government did little to promote economic growth, but it was adequate for maintenance of the economy at a relatively constant level of per capita output.

## West Africa

A more surprising illustration comes from West Africa. One might visualize the economic organization of this region in precolonial times as unusually primitive and custom-bound, with tribal villages existing in economic isolation and following an unchanging production routine. But evidence assembled by A. G. Hopkins (1973) suggests that the reality was rather different.

As of 1800–50, West Africa was sparsely populated. Hours worked were low, varying with the season, but averaging perhaps half a day over the course of the year. This did not reflect a strong preference for leisure but resulted partly from physical debility due to tropical diseases and partly from resource constraints, which limited the opportunity for productive activity. There were substantial concentrations of population. Of the Hausa population in what is now northern Nigeria, about half lived in towns, of which Kano with 30,000 people was the largest. Yorubaland had a dozen towns of 20,000 or more. Ibadan, the principal city, had 70,000 people and city walls with a circumference of 24 miles. There was also much mobility among the population, associated mainly with shifting pasturage of livestock and with trading activities.

Production occurred mainly within the household, support of whose members was an overhead cost that was spread over a variety of activities. There was also a market for nonfamily labor, though this was mainly a slave rather than a hired-labor market. Slavery was a long-established institution, especially in areas where development of an exchange economy had created more employment opportunities than could be met by local free labor. Slaves were preferred because the cost of acquiring and maintaining them was less than the cost of hiring labor for wages.

Agriculture was the basic economic activity, with cereals predominating in the northern savanna and root crops, which yield more calories per acre, predominating in the forest. Cattle raising, an ancient activity, was restricted to areas free of tsetse fly and usually involved migration in search of adequate pasture. The early food crops had come mainly from Asia by way of the Middle East. Through contact with European traders many new crops were introduced, especially from

South America. Successful innovations included corn, cassava, groundnuts, to-
bacco, and cocoa. The crops that survived and spread did so for the good reason
that the value of output exceeded the cost of production. This responsiveness to
change refutes the idea of a static "traditional" economy.

At least seven different methods of cultivation were practiced in different
parts of West Africa, ranging from shifting use of virgin land to permanent,
intensive cultivation. The average length of the fallow period, a good measuring
rod for comparing different systems, seems to have been mainly a function of
population density, availability of fertilizer from animal or other sources, and the
range of crops produced. Permanent cultivation was associated with a rather dense
population, good fertilizer supply, and a variety of crops. Here again we see an
economic adaptation to the environment.

Africans seem to have been quite good farm managers. The charge of primitive technology is based mainly on their limited use of the plow. But the evidence
suggests that this was a rational decision, reflecting the fact that deep plowing was
not suited to fragile tropical soils, or that the plow was too costly relative to
available alternatives, or both. Nor is it accurate to say that productivity was
hampered by "communal tenure" of land. Although land ownership was usually
vested in the village, cultivation rights to particular strips were clearly allocated
among families and could even be inherited.

Regarding industry Hopkins notes in *An Economic History of West Africa*
that "pre-colonial Africa had a range of manufacturing industries which closely
resembled that of pre-industrial societies in other parts of the world . . . based on
clothing, metal working, ceramics, construction, and food processing." Kano
was a major textile center, a kind of Manchester of West Africa. Leather goods
were prominent in cattle-raising areas. Pottery production was widely diffused
throughout the region. While most of these handicraft activities were carried on
within family units, they were often regulated by guild rules that any European
would have recognized as familiar.

The extensive development of trade and markets should be emphasized as an
offset to stereotypes of purely subsistence production. Local trade was carried on
in regular town markets, to which people walked from a radius of ten miles or so,
bringing in foodstuffs and carrying back craft products. Nearby towns arranged to
rotate their market days to avoid overlapping.

Perhaps more surprising, there was an organized network of long trade
routes, covering distances as great as from the Lake Chad area to Dakar or from
Kano to the Mediterranean coast. This long-distance trade usually moved in
caravans, which individual traders could join for part or all of their journey. The
caravans provided protection from bandits and other economies of joint effort.
There were recognized trade centers along these routes for the assembly, breakup,
or reexport of shipments; an elaborate system of local agents and commission men;
banking and credit facilities; even a code of commercial morality. Transport was
by boat along water routes, by head porterage in the forest, by donkeys and camels
in the savanna and desert.

The people who participated in this trade can be classified as:

1. "Target marketers," who made a few trips in the dry season carrying cloth, salt, kola nuts, or whatever, to acquire a certain sum of money for a specific purpose.
2. Regular traders, whose commercial operations were integrated vertically with some specialized production activities. Thus a producer might gradually accumulate a stock of iron implements, weapons, or whatever, and then sell them when market conditions were favorable.
3. Specialized and substantial professional traders, with no connection with production. These could be regarded as business firms, with an established operating routine, a head-office staff, and a network of buying and selling agents scattered along their trade route.
4. Official traders buying or selling on behalf of some royal house. At this stage a high proportion of state revenue came either directly from trade or from taxes levied on traders.

## The Sherpas of Northern Nepal

A word finally on a small but interesting economy still in the extensive-growth stage, one that is perhaps as untouched by modernization as that in any part of the world. Walking through the Sherpa country gives one the impression of having stepped back several centuries to some area of medieval Europe. My expertise on this economy comes from four long treks into the Himalaya, each lasting about five weeks and covering several hundred miles over mountain trails, that I made accompanied only by my wife and a caravan of Sherpa guides and porters. Our guide on these expeditions, Sherpa Ang Lakpa of Khumjung village, is an experienced mountaineer who speaks Tibetan, Sherpa, and Nepali as well as English, French, and German. He was invaluable in putting economic questions for me to villagers and traders and translating their replies, as well as in explaining his own domestic economy.

The Sherpas are descended from Tibetans who from about 1850 onward moved south over the Himalayan passes; they occupy the higher valleys, at altitudes of 8,000 to 15,000 feet. Most of their family labor time (including heavy labor by women as well as men) is spent in food production. Millet and other coarse grains can be grown in the lower altitudes; potatoes, almost as important to the Sherpas as to the Irish, can be grown at 12,000 feet. The yak, which good Buddhists must not kill or eat, is in all other ways a most useful animal. It provides milk, blood (drawn from the veins, as the Masai do in Africa, and mixed with porridge to provide animal protein), and hair (the main raw material for cloth spinning and weaving).

Almost everything that is consumed is home-produced. Clothing, Tibetan-style boots, and carpets are woven in the household on simple hand looms. The sturdy, Swiss-style houses needed to withstand winter weather are built by the householder with the help of neighbors and a few specialized artisans in the village. Recreation and other "services" are also home-produced. They include village feasts, which each family is obligated to provide in turn, depleting its liquidity for some years to come; and religious festivals at local monasteries, which the villages support mainly by contributions of food.

Trade with lower regions to the south is severely constrained by lack of transport. The terrain is so steep and broken that it is not feasible to build roads suited to wheeled vehicles. Whatever moves must move over footpaths on the backs of people, donkeys, or crossbred cattle used as pack animals. So in the short (in miles) journey from southern to northern Nepal, a kilo of rice or wheat doubles in price; and a glass window (one of the few signs of Sherpa affluence) or a large piece of lumber carried on a porter's back from Kathmandu triples in price.

Some rice and wheat does come in. And villagers from lower altitudes also bring chickens, eggs, goats, and other supplies to the great weekly market at Namche Bazaar, where local people sit on the hillside and estimate the day's prices by the number of sellers approaching up the valley. The only other significant imports to Sherpa land are metal tools and cooking utensils, bits of hardware for door hinges, and salt.

Money is widely used, mainly in the form of Nepalese rupees, though the black-market value of foreign currencies is also well known. Economic motivation is pervasive. People know to a penny the difference between the price of a commodity in one area and another, and if the spread is sufficient to cover transport costs, goods will move. Income differences are sufficient to be noted and envied. Everyone is eager to have a bit more land, glass windows and copper cooking utensils in the home, an additional yak, or a crossbred pack animal that can be used to supplement family income.

As one lives with these honest, kindly, cheerful people, one is bound to ask, "In what way are they poor?" Any comparative tabulation of worldwide per capita income would put them near the bottom of the list. What does this mean? They are eating reasonably well, their clothing is adequate for the climate, their houses are substantial and durable. Education is still almost absent. Few adult Sherpas have ever been in a school, and such language and arithmetical skills as they have are self-taught. Health conditions are also poor, with tuberculosis and goiter especially common. There is only one small, foreign-financed hospital with two doctors for all the villages in the Everest region. Life expectancy is short. In these respects the Sherpas are indeed poor, though not as badly off as the gross national product (GNP) figures would suggest.

Examples could be multiplied—from India, from Java, from Egypt, and elsewhere. But the cases cited here are perhaps sufficient to dispel misconceptions about the pre–turning point economy. Production does *not* consist only of grubbing food from the soil. People produce and consume a wide range of goods and services. The economy is *not* uncommercial and unmonetized. A considerable percentage of output is exchanged among households. Local trade is always important, and long-distance trade is often quite important. Individual and family calculations are *not* "uneconomic." There is abundant evidence that poor and illiterate people can make precise calculations of economic advantage. The economy is *not* unresponsive to innovation, as shown particularly by the spread of new crops imported from other parts of the world and the gradual intensification of cultivation systems.

POPULATION AND FOOD SUPPLY

## Population Growth

During the era of extensive growth, population is increasing by definition; and this increase begins very early. Durand (in *Population Problems*, 1967) estimates that population was growing at a low rate almost everywhere in the world from at least 1750 onward. (A possible exception is tropical Africa, for which estimates before 1900 are quite dubious.) Growth rates were low by modern standards. In Europe, the average growth rate was about 0.7 percent per year from 1800 to 1850 and 0.8 percent from 1850 to 1900. Kuznets's estimate (in Easterlin, 1980) for the less-developed countries places their average population growth at 0.35 percent from 1800 to 1850 and 0.56 percent from 1850 to 1900.

The great killers are famine, war, and plague. Where these are somewhat under control, population tends to grow through a modest excess of births over deaths. During the extensive-growth stage of development, the fertility rate is mainly the result of uncontrolled reproduction. People are not sure that they will have as many surviving children as they would prefer to have. In Easterlin's terminology, the desired number of children, $C_d$, is greater than the natural fertility rate, $C_n$; so the former is dominant, and there is no incentive for population control.

To speak of a "natural fertility rate" does not imply that it is a universal constant determined by biology alone. Even the uncontrolled birth rate is influenced by such things as: (1) the percentage of women who marry; (2) average age at marriage, which varies presently from around 30 in Ireland to 25 in the United States to 20 in tropical Africa; (3) the rate at which fecundity declines with age; (4) the average interval between births, which is influenced by social factors such as breast-feeding customs and taboos on intercourse during breast-feeding, and so may vary from less than two years to more than three years; (5) the probability of husband or wife dying before the end of the child-bearing period. Because of these factors, uncontrolled birth rates range from about 35 to 55 per thousand.

The mortality rate is somewhat influenced by economic factors. Famine, traditionally an important cause of death, has been gradually eliminated by reductions in the cost of transporting food within and among countries. More recently, improvements in nutrition, sanitation, and literacy have reduced child mortality from diarrhea and other diseases. To a large extent, however, the determinants of mortality are exogenous, related to the progress of medical science; and this progress is somewhat discontinuous. Thus after a gradual sag of mortality rates up to 1914 we see a marked drop after 1920 and another marked drop after 1945.

Although in general we shall argue for similarity between "early developers" and "late developers," the population growth rate is one respect in which the timing of a country's turning point makes a decided difference. Countries that reached the turning point before 1914 did so when the population growth rate was still low, typically below 1 percent. For output to accelerate sufficiently to outrace population and initiate intensive growth was thus no great feat.

But since 1920, and especially since 1945, population growth in third-world countries has accelerated sharply. Medical progress has impinged on every country, regardless of its income level or growth rate. For countries already well launched on intensive growth, including most of Latin America and parts of East and Southeast Asia, high population growth rates did not pose an insuperable problem. But for latecomers, those still in the extensive-growth phase in 1945, the problem of getting started has been formidable. This is one reason that some of the post-1945 turning points remain precarious and that some countries have not yet reached the turning point.

## Growth of Food Supply

We have defined extensive growth as a situation in which population growth is matched by growth of national output and in particular of food supply. When we see population growing, how do we know that this second condition is met? The data for some of the larger third-world countries, such as Brazil, India, China, and Indonesia, have been worked over with considerable care. Typically, studies suggest that food output per capita was either stationary or rising very slowly in the premodern period. Usually, however, we have to resort to negative reasoning. *If* population growth had been accompanied by marked deterioration of living standards, one would expect this deterioration to have been reported by informed observers. While reports of short-term hardships arising from drought and other natural disasters are common in the literature, reports of a secular decline in living standards are rare. In general, growing populations manage to feed themselves at near-stationary levels.

How is this feat accomplished? Least interesting, though very important historically, is the simple extension of the cultivated area. As of 1900, most of the countries in our sample still had reserves of unused land, and some countries of Africa and South America still do. The spreading out of population over a larger area, with at least a proportionate increase in agricultural output, is familiar from American history and presents no analytical problems.

More interesting is intensification of cultivation, which tends to accompany acreage expansion and becomes dominant when the frontier finally closes. Using length of the fallow period as an indicator of intensity, one can lay out a spectrum of cultivation systems ranging from slash-and-burn through bush fallow to short fallow, annual cropping with no fallow period, and multicropping. Ester Boserup (1964, 1981) has argued persuasively that movement along this spectrum is an endogenous result of population growth. The population increase that requires larger food supplies also tends to produce them by bringing about a shift toward more intensive land use. She uses cross-section analysis across countries to test the relation between population density and the cultivation system, with good results.

More intensive cultivation systems, of course, require larger factor inputs per unit of land. Labor inputs present no problem. More mouths to feed are accompanied by more hands to cultivate, a state that has reached a high point in Chinese or Javanese rice growing, which resembles gardening more than farming. When the soil is no longer allowed to recuperate through fallow periods, larger fertilizer inputs become necessary—at this stage, mainly organic rather than chemical fertilizer. Multicropping, and even annual cropping in areas of deficient rainfall, typically requires large investments of labor in drainage and irrigation facilities. The historical literature reports heavy investment in irrigation in the nineteenth century in Egypt, Iraq, Sri Lanka, India, China, and Java.

By such methods it is possible to raise crop yields *per acre* in the most intensive cultivation systems several times over yields in less intensive systems. Yield *per farm worker* will tend to fall, but perhaps not very much. Ishikawa (1981) has made cross-country studies of rice cultivation in which yield per hectare on the vertical axis is charted against available hectares per farm worker on the horizontal axis. The results conform quite closely to a rectangular hyperbola, sometimes called an "Ishikawa curve." Data for the same country, such as Japan or Taiwan, in successive time periods show a similar pattern. Yield per hectare moves upward to the left along the Ishikawa curve as land availability decreases.

A further possibility for increasing yield in changes in the agricultural product mix. Potatoes and other root crops yield substantially more calories per acre than do most grain crops, and thus a reallocation of land among crops can raise caloric availability. Another way in which densely populated countries adjust is through de-emphasis of livestock production. Boserup finds a strong inverse relation between population density and pasture area/cultivated area and livestock/person ratios. Large animals are a very inefficient way of converting acreage into calories, though pigs and chickens are somewhat more efficient. Densely populated areas tend to get a high proportion of their animal protein from fish.

Several of these possibilities are indicated by the experience of China, which was summarized in the previous section. Over the six centuries before 1949, output per cultivated acre roughly doubled. This was accomplished through a combination of seed improvement, introduction of new crops, extension of double-cropping made possible by irrigation, and an increase of labor and fertilizer inputs per acre. There was technical change, but of a gradual and traditional sort. "Modern" technical change, in which yields are raised rapidly by a combination of seed improvement, application of chemical fertilizers and pesticides, and improved cultivation methods, was not important in any of our countries during the extensive-growth era.

Industrial output grows along with population and agricultural output, and there is a gradual shift in the locus of manufacturing activity from the household to specialized workshops and cottage industry. Since clothing is a major consumer good, textiles tend to take the lead in this process. The putting-out system, in which a merchant supplies materials to home spinners and weavers and then collects and markets their product, is familiar to readers of European economic history; but it was by no means confined to that continent. Quite similar systems existed in China, India, and many other third-world countries. One typically finds in addition to textiles an array of other handicraft industries supplying household necessities.

Handicraft production in turn gives way gradually to factory production, with textiles and raw-material processing in the lead. Handicraft products are often forced to compete first with imported factory goods and later on with the output of domestic factories. Whether factory production appears during the period of extensive growth depends on the era we are discussing. In the substantial number of countries that reached the turning point before 1900, factories were almost absent at the turning point and did not become important for several decades thereafter. This is why it is wrong to take the onset of industrialization as marking the beginning of intensive growth for these countries. But when we come to the years 1900–50, by which time modern industrial techniques were increasingly well known throughout the world, we find considerable development of factory production in countries such as Egypt, Turkey, India, and China when they were still in the extensive-growth phase. And since 1950 efforts to initiate intensive growth have been strongly identified with forced-draft industrial development.

The volume of internal trade and transport grows with the volume of production, and may indeed grow somewhat faster, as urban centers develop and households begin to shed some of their nonagricultural functions. Trade networks are elaborated and perfected. Further, as European traders voyaged around the world from 1500 onward, most of the countries discussed here developed some external trade, typically involving exchange of primary products for manufactured consumer goods. The volume of such trade may have grown somewhat faster than domestic output, but it was still marginal rather than central to the economy. Only after about 1850 do we observe, in one country after another, a marked rise in the export/GDP ratio, which I shall argue in chapter 3 was often important in initiating growth.

The public sector remained small. Nineteenth-century governments, whether indigenous or colonial, collected only a small percentage of national income, mainly from head taxes, land taxes, and trade taxes. Expenditures were mainly for the military, the civil service, and consumption of the ruling group, with little remaining for economic or social purposes. But there was some building of roads, railroads, ports, and warehouses for trade and military uses. Interestingly enough, some colonial governments were more active on this front than were most independent countries.

Since national accounts are typically lacking for the period of extensive growth, we cannot say what is happening to the sectoral composition of output or the sectoral distribution of the labor force. But it is a reasonable surmise that the economy shows little structural change. One implication of extensive growth is that part of the growth in the labor force is being absorbed in nonagricultural activities. Extension of settlement over a larger land area means some increase in transport requirements. Growth of total output and income means more people are engaged in trade and trade-related activities. The service sector is large and expansible, though at this stage it involves mainly personal services. We have already noted the gradual transfer of some types of manufacturing and repair work from the household to independent artisans and also some increased absorption of family labor time in manufacturing for the market, as under the putting-out system.

In all these ways the demand for labor is growing, and it may well grow as rapidly as the available labor supply. The "surplus-labor" economy, so prominent in recent development literature, had not yet appeared on a substantial scale. Only in Egypt, Java, and some regions of India and China were there complaints of overpopulation. In other third-world countries, and especially in Africa and Latin America, population density was low relative to land resources. As intensive growth got under way, the common complaint was of labor scarcity.

THREE ANALYTICAL PROBLEMS

Absence of Economic Change?

The economic literature contains several models of an essentially changeless economy—the classical stationary state, Schumpeter's "circular flow of economic life," the Walrasian general equilibrium system. In these systems population, capital stock, and technology are constant, and the economy grinds out the same menu of goods period after period. It is worth emphasizing that economies in the extensive-growth era do not correspond to any of these models. Output per capita is unchanged in the sense of fluctuating about a level trend line. But other types of economic change, usually gradual and undramatic, pervade the economy.

Numerous examples of such change were given in the previous section. Population is spreading out gradually over a larger land area—from Java to the outer islands of Indonesia, from central China to the north and southwest, from Upper Burma to Lower Burma, from Buenos Aires to the pampas of Argentina,

and so on. In agriculture, cultivation methods and crop mix are usually changing. There may also be institutional changes, such as clarification of individual
titles to land, which was an important nineteenth-century development in some
countries. There is an elaboration of handicraft production of manufactures, sometimes under the auspices of merchant entrepreneurs. There is gradual improvement of roads, ports, and other infrastructure. There is growing contact with other
economies along seacoast fringes.

These changes stand out particularly in the "late developers"—India,
China, Indonesia, Egypt, Turkey Iraq, Iran. Although per capita income in these
countries was not appreciably higher in 1950 than in 1900, in other respects their
economies had changed significantly: important governmental changes, accelerated population growth, better infrastructure, an enlarged and changed pattern of
exports, more-intensive land use usually accompanied by irrigation development,
even the beginnings of factory industry.

## "Change without Change"

How can the economy grow in absolute size, and even undergo the significant
changes just noted, without any appreciable uptrend in per capita income? By
previous economic reasoning, population growth *was* expected to change per
capita income, usually in a negative direction. In early classical models, any
temporary improvement in living standards led to more rapid population growth,
which forced a return to the subsistence level of the stationary state. Malthus, the
classical economist most concerned with population, argued that man's reproduc-
tive capacity would lead naturally to a doubling of population in each generation.
But food output can be increased only at a slower rate. So, unless the population
growth rate is held down by voluntary restraint, it will be cut back forcibly by
famine and disease.

Why has historical reality not conformed very closely to the Malthusian
predictions? One reason, less important today than in the past, is widespread
availability of uncultivated land of good quality. Malthus, writing in the English
context, naturally thought in terms of a fully settled country. A second reason,
ruled out by the implicit classical assumption of static technology, is the possibility of technical progress in agriculture. The Boserup hypothesis that population growth itself tends to generate such changes is relevant here. Further, the
agglomeration of population may generate modest economies of scale in transport,
trade, and small-scale industrial activities. If Adam Smith was right about the
relation between market size and division of labor, one might expect a gradual rise
of productivity in the nonagricultural sectors, perhaps sufficient to offset any
tendency toward diminishing returns in agriculture as intensity of cultivation
increases. These considerations may help to explain the deviation of actual economic growth from Malthusian predictions.

## The Question of Preconditions

To what extent can developments during the period of extensive growth be regarded as a preparation for, or a prerequisite for, the turning point to intensive growth?

The answer depends on how the question is put. One could ask: does extensive growth tend to develop naturally, almost automatically, into intensive growth, so that from existence of the former one can predict eventual appearance of the latter? I suspect that the answer to this question is no. There seems no reason to believe that per capita income *must* begin to rise or that extensive growth could not continue indefinitely.

But suppose one asks instead: are developments during this era of extensive growth *helpful* at later stages of growth? Is the economy in some sense better prepared for takeoff at the end of the period than it was at the beginning? The answer to this more modest question may well be yes. Some events of this period are decidedly helpful to later growth. In regard to Europe, Eric Jones (1981) has emphasized that a great deal of gradual change was going on before the so-called modern period. This stage-setting was spread over several centuries. It included: the solidification of nation-states and some increase in the optimum size of states; the growing autonomy of the market economy from the political systems, achieved partly through the spread of rural industry outside the control of the urban guilds; the growth of what Jones terms "ghost acreage" in the newly discovered continents overseas, which greatly increased the land per man available to Europeans; and creeping changes in technology, partly by trial and error, but increasingly as the result of more abstract speculation. "Small but productive technical changes were constantly being made in the more advanced regions, though many are scarcely discernible in the documented sources and are individually too minor to figure among the stylized facts of technical change during the Industrial Revolution, which rears up as a cliff face in the textbooks where it should emerge instead from swelling foothills" (p. 65).

The same view is warranted, I think, for most third-world countries. Important conditioning factors during the period of extensive growth include: (1) nation-building, which in many countries is a recent and precarious process, still going on with varying degrees of success; (2) small technical changes that add up to what we might call "the importance of the inconspicuous"; (3) changes in crops, water-control systems, and cultivation methods, which enable food output to at least keep up with population; (4) gradual reduction of transport costs and extension of long-distance trade; (5) growth of manufacturing production outside the household, or even within the household through the putting-out system.

These factors are perhaps especially important for countries that have *recently* embarked on intensive growth after a long prior exposure to the world economy. For example, India in 1947 had a tradition of national unity and democratic government, a well-staffed civil service, a substantial educational system, much physical infrastructure, a long tradition of handicraft manufacturing, and the beginnings of factory industry, notably in textiles. Some of these things could be said also of China, Pakistan, Egypt, Turkey, and other recent developers. They were taking off, not from a situation of stagnation, but from an economy already visibly in motion.

# 3

## The Timing of Turning Points

Modern economic growth began in the United Kingdom in the mideighteenth century, and in France in the late eighteenth century. By 1850 it had spread to most of northern and western Europe, North America, and Australia. Southern and Eastern Europe were to come along later. Western economists and historians often assumed that nothing much was happening in the third world, Japan being regarded as an exception to the general rule. The other countries of Asia, Africa, and Latin America were seen as marginal—mere suppliers of raw materials to the developing industrial countries. Thus when Western economists turned their attention to third-world countries after 1945, they assumed that the era of economic development was just beginning for the rest of the world. The countries of the third world were all lined up at the starting gate, preparing to "take off" into an era of sustained growth.

This chronology, in which Europe and North America develop very early and other countries follow only after a century-long delay, is seriously distorted. First, turning points within Europe itself were spread out over a period of about two centuries. Very roughly, intensive growth spread from northwest to southeast. France, Belgium, and Switzerland were early followers of the United Kingdom, their intensive growth dating from about 1800. By the 1830s Austria, the states of western Germany, and the United States had joined the growth procession. The Scandinavian countries and Australia came along in midcentury, Canada around 1870. Intensive growth in Hungary, Russia, and Italy seems to have been under way by the 1880s; that in Poland and Czechoslovakia, which did not exist as independent countries before World War I, can be dated from the 1920s (though the Bohemian region of Czechoslovakia was already growing in the nineteenth century). Not until after 1945 were Rumania, Bulgaria, and Yugoslavia drawn strongly into the growth current. The spread of intensive growth from the initial "core" to peripheral areas to the south and east was gradual and long drawn out.

Meanwhile, a similarly long drawn out process was under way on other continents. Intensive growth began in Chile about 1840, in Argentina about 1860. By 1900 most other Latin American countries, as well as Japan and most of

Southeast Asia, had joined the procession. In Africa, intensive growth began in the 1890s under colonial auspices, the present African countries being in fact colonial creations. Intensive growth in Korea dates from 1910, in Zambia, Morocco, and Venezuela from the 1920s. Another important group, including the Asian giants, India and China, as well as Egypt, Turkey, Iraq, Iran, Pakistan, and Indonesia, embarked on intensive growth only after 1945. And seven of the countries in our sample still have not done so, remaining in the extensive-growth era. In the third world the sequence of turning points has been spread out over a century and a half and is by no means complete. Thus we see that the procession of turning points in Europe *overlaps* heavily with the corresponding procession in the third world.

My early dating of turning points for most third-world countries is admittedly controversial and will raise several questions in readers' minds. The most substantial of these relate, first, to the fact that more than half of these countries were still colonies at my turning-point date. Can a country really embark on intensive growth under colonial auspices? Second, my datings depend rather heavily on an increase in the growth rate of primary exports from the country in question. It has sometimes been argued that primary exports are of doubtful benefit to a developing country and do not provide a reliable basis for sustained growth.

The evidence suggests that export expansion usually is a major factor in initiating intensive growth; but there are exceptions, and the reasons for these need to be explored. The best procedure is perhaps to set forth the chronology of turning points as I visualize it and then to consider possible objections and qualifications.

TABLE 1    A Chronology of Turning Points

| 1840 | Chile | 1900 | Uganda |
|------|-------|------|--------|
| 1850 | Malaysia | 1900 | Zimbabwe |
| 1850 | Thailand | 1910 | Korea |
| 1860 | Argentina | 1920 | Morocco |
| 1870 | Burma | 1925 | Venezuela |
| 1876 | Mexico | 1925 | Zambia |
| 1880 | Algeria | 1947 | India |
| 1880 | Brazil | 1947 | Pakistan |
| 1880 | Japan | 1949 | China |
| 1880 | Peru | 1950 | Iran |
| 1880 | Sri Lanka | 1950 | Iraq |
| 1885 | Colombia | 1950 | Turkey |
| 1890 | Nigeria | 1952 | Egypt |
| 1895 | Ghana | 1965 | Indonesia |
| 1895 | Ivory Coast | — | Afghanistan |
| 1895 | Kenya | — | Bangladesh |
| 1895 | Taiwan | — | Ethiopia |
| 1900 | Cuba | — | Mozambique |
| 1900 | Philippines | — | Nepal |
| 1900 | Tanzania | — | Sudan |
| | | — | Zaire |

## THE CHRONOLOGY OF TURNING POINTS

The dates listed in table 1 are subject to the qualifications noted in chapter 1 about the use of a single year. The turning point is actually a period of a decade or so around the cited year, during which one observes a significant and continuing rise in per capita income.

The striking fact emerging from the table is that about two-thirds of the countries that have thus far reached a turning point had done so by 1914. Between 1914 and 1945, on the other hand, only three countries appear on the list. After 1945 the procession speeds up again, with eight countries reaching the turning point soon thereafter.

I shall argue that this chronology stems from three major epochs in the world economy, whose main features will be reviewed briefly.

### World Economic Boom, 1850–1914

It is clear in retrospect that the 1850–1914 era was unusually favorable to worldwide diffusion of economic growth. Output in the early-developing countries of Europe and North America was rising rapidly, and with it their demand for imports of primary products. Kuznets (1966) estimates the median growth rate of output in these countries from 1860 to 1914 at about 3 percent per year, which meant a median growth of about 2 percent a year in per capita terms.

Rapid economic growth in Europe and North America opened up the possibility of enlarged trade with other continents. But this possibility could scarcely have been realized without an improvement and cheapening of transport. This involved replacement of sailing ships by steam-driven steel ships, which reduced ocean-freight rates by 1913 to about 30 percent of their 1870 level; a worldwide railroad boom, which peaked in the years 1870–1914 and which produced even more spectacular reductions in overland transport costs; and building of a worldwide telegraph network linking would-be sellers and buyers. Completion of the Suez Canal in 1869 was a particularly important development for Asian countries trading with Europe.

Available estimates of growth in the volume of international trade have been analyzed by Kuznets (1967). They show the sum of exports and imports growing at an average rate of 50.3 percent per decade from 1850 to 1880 and 39.5 percent per decade from 1881 to 1913. The ratio of world trade to world output was thus rising quite rapidly. Kuznets estimates that this ratio had reached 33 percent by 1913.

Trade was of course dominated by the countries of Europe and North America, which accounted for about three-quarters of combined exports and imports. Latin America, Africa, and Asia accounted for about 20 percent of trade in 1876–80 and 22 percent in 1913, not far from their proportion in recent decades. The implication of these figures is that third-world countries were keeping up with the general pace of world trade. This conclusion is confirmed by the investigations of Lewis (1969), who finds that the volume of tropical exports grew at 3.6 percent per year from 1883 to 1913. Agricultural exports grew a bit more slowly than this, but mineral exports grew more quickly. Indeed, during this period total exports from the tropical countries grew at almost exactly the same rate as industrial production in the advanced countries. Although terms of trade between primary products and manufactures show short-term fluctuations, Lewis (1970) concludes that there was no appreciable change in terms over this period as a whole.

The third-world countries that embarked on intensive growth before World War I fall into three groups.

1. *Latin America.* All the Latin American countries in our sample, with the exception of Venezuela. The turning-point dates in most cases mark the beginning of political stability after the prolonged civil wars that followed independence. Growth was invariably export-led, the nature of the exports varying from case to case. Argentina and Chile were able to grow and export wool, wheat, meat, and other temperate-zone products. Brazil relied on tropical products, initially sugar, with coffee becoming dominant from the 1840s onward. Coffee also dominated the early export trade of Colombia. Minerals were important in Chile—at first nitrates, later copper. Minerals dominated Mexico's nineteenth-century exports, though agricultural products, cattle, and timber gradually grew in importance. Peru also had a combination of agricultural and mineral exports. Cuba was a sugar island. But everywhere exports, directed mainly toward European and North American markets, were the key to economic expansion.

2. *Asia.* Four of the Asian countries that were drawn into the world export boom lie in an arc—from Ceylon through Burma and Malaya to Thailand.* Their turning points can be dated generally from the 1850s, though Ceylon had large and growing coffee exports from the 1830s onward. In Burma and Thailand a rising flow of rice exports came mainly from peasant producers expanding into uncultivated land, a pattern to be repeated later in West Africa. In Malaya the early export product was tin, produced mainly by relatively small entrepreneurs of Chinese origin, but by 1900 rubber had emerged as a second major product. Ceylon's exports came initially from large foreign-owned plantations—coffee plantations from 1830–70, tea plantations after the coffee trees had been ruined by plant disease. Toward the end of the century, however, smallholder production of coconuts, rubber, and other crops became increasingly important, and by 1913 the export list was quite diversified.

Next, there is the case of Japan, so well documented in the literature that details would be superfluous. But it is worth noting that Japan, like the other countries listed, showed a consistently strong export performance. Exports plus

_____

*In some cases the name of a country after independence differs from the name during the colonial era. In such cases I have used the old name (Ceylon, Malaya, Tanganyika, and so on) in discussing the earlier period and the new name (Sri Lanka, Malaysia, Tanzania) in discussing events since independence.

imports were about 10 percent of GNP in the 1870s, but had risen to 30 percent by 1910–13. Over the years 1881–1914, Japanese exports grew about twice as rapidly as world exports. Up to 1900 Japan's export growth is mainly the story of raw silk, after 1900 mainly the story of cotton textiles.

Taiwan and the Philippines round out the Asian experience. Taiwan was ceded to Japan after China's defeat in the Sino-Japanese war of 1894–95. Japan energetically set out to turn the island into a rice bowl for the home country. The Philippines passed under American control after Spain's defeat in the Spanish-American War of 1898. There followed a period of rapid export-led growth, dominated by sugar and aided by a preferential trade agreement with the United States.

3. *Africa.* Toward the end of the century several areas of Africa were drawn into the intensive-growth process. Algeria in North Africa; Nigeria, Ghana, and Ivory Coast in West Africa; Kenya, Uganda, and Tanganyika (Tanzania) in East Africa; and Southern Rhodesia (Zimbabwe) in Central Africa. To speak of these as "countries" is to speak of colonial creations. Europeans drew the boundaries, established unified administration over numerous tribal areas, and created an impression of nationhood that, although it took on some substance over the years, was never as strong as that inherited from the ancient kingdoms of Asia.

Most of the Asian and Latin American countries mentioned participated in the pre-1914 boom for periods of forty to sixty years. The new African colonies were latecomers who participated for a generation or less. They nevertheless got in on the tail end of the boom. Their exports rose sharply up to 1914, giving them an initial momentum that they never entirely lost. Wheat, fruits, and wine from Algeria; palm products, cocoa, coffee, and timber from West Africa; cereals from Kenya, cotton from Uganda, sisal and coffee from Tanganyika; cereals, gold, and other minerals from Southern Rhodesia—all flowed into international trade in growing volume. Exports from Ghana, Nigeria, Ivory Coast, and Uganda came almost entirely from African smallholders, who brought additional land under cultivation in the pattern observed earlier in Southeast Asia. In Algeria, Kenya, and Southern Rhodesia, on the other hand, substantial white settlement created dualistic economies in which most of the exports came from European-owned farms.

## The Longest Depression, 1914–45

This phrase, borrowed from Lewis (1978a), is adequately descriptive. Nineteen fourteen to 1945 was a bleak period for the world economy, marked by two world wars, the Great Depression, and a marked slowdown in the growth of world production and trade. The growth rate of industrial production in the "developed" countries fell from 3.6 percent in 1883–1913 to 2.7 percent in 1913–29 and 1.3 percent in 1929–38. This drop is significant in view of Lewis's finding that the growth rate of primary exports from tropical countries is closely related to growth of industrial production in the advanced economies. And in fact the growth rate of tropical exports fell from 3.7 percent per year in 1883–1913 to 3.2 percent in 1913–29 and 1.9 percent in 1929–37. This decline in export volume was accompanied by a mild sagging of the terms of trade of primary products against manufactures even before 1929 and by a sharp drop after 1929. The import capacity of third-world countries was sharply reduced.

Under these depressed conditions, countries that had been growing quite rapidly before 1914 now grew more slowly. It is significant, too, that only a few additional countries reached the turning point during this period, and these cases can be attributed to special circumstances. Korea was formally taken over by Japan in 1910 and, as in the earlier case of Taiwan, Japan set about to develop the country as an auxiliary to the Japanese economy. A French protectorate was established in Morocco in 1912 as part of a deal among the European powers, and effective control over most of the territory had been gained by 1920. Here, as earlier in Algeria, French settlers in effect implanted a new, "modern" economy on top of the indigenous economy, initiating a growth process whose benefits went disproportionately to the Europeans.

In Venezuela, which had remaind a stagnant backwater dominated by military dictators and an agricultural oligarchy, the discovery of oil in the early 1920s set off a rapid transformation of both the economy and the political structure. Venezuela was the first great oil exporter and remains a key member of OPEC, which it took the initiative in founding in the 1960s. In Zambia (then Northern Rhodesia), rich copper deposits began to be exploited by foreign-owned companies in the late 1920s. While these properties have now passed from foreign to national ownership, copper remains a dominant factor in the economy.

## The Greatest Boom, 1945–73

The evolution of the world economy after World War II is still fresh in mind and can be reviewed very briefly. The years 1945–73 saw an unprecedented boom in world production and trade, a "second golden age" with growth rates well above those of the "first golden age" of 1850–1914. The average annual growth rate of GNP in the OECD countries from 1950 to 1973 was 4.9 percent, compared with an 1870–1913 average of 2.5 percent and a 1913–50 figure of 1.9 percent. These high output rates—plus lowering of trade barriers, plus continued reduction of transport costs (supertankers, container ships, jet aircraft, great expansion of road mileage and truck transport)—produced an even faster growth in the volume of international trade. Angus Maddison (1982) shows the export volume of the OECD countries rising at 8.6 percent per year from 1950 to 1973. Thus export/GNP ratios rose substantially.

Exports from third-world countries, while still growing rapidly by historical standards, grew somewhat less rapidly than developed-country exports, with the result that their percentage of world exports fell from 25.3 percent to 17.7 percent.

There was some diversification of the export mix. Manufactured goods formed only 7.6 percent of third-world exports in 1955, but by 1970 their share had risen to 16.7 percent (and the percentage was to double again by 1980). Meanwhile exports of foodstuffs had fallen from 36.7 percent to 26.5 percent of the total, reflecting not only demand constraints but also increasing domestic food consumption associated with population growth and rising per capita incomes. The great grain-surplus areas are now the United States, Canada, Australia, and Europe. Thus the old distinction between "developed" exporters of manufactures and "less-developed" exporters of primary products has become increasingly blurred. The terms of trade between primary products and manufactures show no marked trend over the period 1945–73.

The boom crested in 1973, and the median growth rate in the OECD countries from 1973 to 1980 fell to about half its previous level—in fact, to almost precisely the rate that had prevailed from 1870 to 1913. There was a corresponding turnaround in world trade. Maddison (1982) shows the average annual growth of OECD exports falling from 8.6 percent in 1950–73 to 4.8 percent in 1973–79. World exports grew even more slowly, at 4.0 percent per year.

Different groups of third-world countries fared quite differently in the 1973–80 period: (1) oil exporters did very well in income terms, though not always well in terms of economic policy; (2) countries that had established a substantial industrial base by 1973, often grouped together as "newly industrializing countries" or NICs, have also done well—their median growth rate since 1973 is well above that of the OECD countries; (3) other oil-importing countries in the third world have found their growth rates retarded and have been kept afloat partly by short-term borrowing, which can scarcely continue to increase at recent rates; (4) countries that had not yet reached the turning point by 1973 have fared worst, and their chances of reaching it now appear even bleaker than before.

The main effect of the 1945–73 golden age was to speed up growth in countries that had already embarked on intensive growth at various points between 1850 and 1950. Virtually all countries—the OECD countries, Eastern Europe and the Soviet Union, as well as third-world countries that had already reached the turning point—experienced a sharp increase in GNP growth rates. In the euphoria of this period it was perhaps natural to suppose that third-world growth before 1950 had been negligible. But what had actually happened, for the nineteenth-century and early-twentieth-century developers, was that a previously moderate growth rate of per capita income accelerated after 1950 to a markedly higher level.

However, the view that "development began in 1950," while largely illusory, is not entirely so. Eight countries reached the turning point in the 1950–80 period, including China and India, plus Pakistan and Indonesia. In both China and undivided India one could make a case for a slight rise in per capita income from 1900 to 1940. But the increase, if present at all, is so slight that in my judgment the turning point for India and Pakistan should be dated from independence in 1947 and for China from the revolution of 1949.

There is some ambiguity about the correct dating of turning points for four of the eight countries—Egypt, Turkey, Iraq, and Iran. These countries experienced some political and economic modernization from the 1920s onward. But the 1929 depression and the 1939 war followed so soon afterwards that they had scarcely made a significant beginning before 1945. It seems most reasonable, then, to locate their turning points in the postwar period.

The case of Indonesia is also complex and somewhat ambiguous. Exports from Indonesia rose from 1880 to 1930 at a quite respectable rate. But to an unusual degree these exports came from foreign-owned mines and plantations, and a large share of the proceeds remained in foreign hands. Particularly in densely populated Java, the benefits to the local population seem to have been meager. As a matter of judgment, then, I prefer to locate Indonesia's turning point after the achievement of independence. Even then, GNP per capita did not begin to rise perceptibly until the overthrow of President Sukarno and installation of the present regime in the mid-1960s.

## Some Laggards

I note finally that seven countries in our sample remain in the phase of extensive growth and show no sign of a sustained rise in per capita income. These countries are Afghanistan, Nepal, Bangladesh, Ethiopia, Sudan, Mozambique, and Zaire. There does not seem to be any single reason for their failure to achieve intensive growth. Rather, failure results from varying combinations of geographic remoteness (Afghanistan, Nepal, most of Ethiopia, Zaire, and Sudan), absence of transport facilities and other infrastructure (all seven countries except Bangladesh), internal political turmoil (absent only in Nepal and post-1970 Sudan), the flight of colonial authorities with no real preparation for independence (Mozambique, Zaire), primitive government (Afghanistan, Ethiopia, Nepal), and massive misgovernment (Zaire).

In the bleaker post-1973 environment these countries, and some smaller countries in similar plight, will have serious difficulty in reaching the turning point. The end of the growth-diffusion story is not yet in sight.

### THE QUESTION OF TIMING

The most intriguing question in growth economics is why a turning point occurs in a particular country at a particular time. Why, under the favorable world conditions of 1850–1914, did some countries embark on intensive growth while others did not? Why was this true once more during the boom of 1945–73? Why have turning points been spread out over more than a century, and why in some countries have they not yet occurred?

A review of the country histories assembled as part of this exercise suggests two clues. First, the turning point is almost always associated with some significant political event. In only four of our 41 countries does this seem not to have been true. Second, the turning point is usually associated with a marked rise in exports. Although rising world demand impinges on all countries, each country differs in its ability to make an appropriate production response. This point will be explored further in a later section.

Among "significant political events" the most interesting cases, though not the largest in number, involve a transfer of power within the country from a less-progressive to a more-progressive regime. Cases that fall under this heading include: installation of the modernizing ruler Rama IV as king of Thailand (1851); the Meiji Restoration in Japan (1868); collapse of the Ottoman Empire and emergence of Kemal Atatürk as ruler of Turkey (early 1920s); emergence of Iraq from the Ottoman Empire as an independent state under British tutelage (early 1920s); installation of the Pahlevi dynasty in Iran (1925); the communist-led revolution in China (1949); overthrow of the monarchy and installation of President Nasser in Egypt (1956); overthrow of President Sukarno and installation of President Suharto in Indonesia (1967).

In Latin America, independence in most countries was followed by a prolonged period of recurring civil war, lasting as late as 1876 in Mexico and 1885 in Colombia. The turning point usually dates from the emergence at long last of a stable government able to exercise effective control of the country for an extended period.

Most numerous are the cases in which intensive growth can be dated from the time of colonization by a foreign power: namely, the ten European-created African countries listed earlier plus Burma, Malaysia, Taiwan, Korea, Cuba, and the Philippines (the last two involving transfer from one colonial power to another rather than fresh colonization). Granting all necessary qualifications about distribution of the increased income from growth, the fact of increased capacity to produce can scarcely be questioned.

In two cases—India and Pakistan—initiation of intensive growth was roughly synchronous with decolonization. Finally, there are four cases (Ceylon, Brazil, Venezuela, and Peru) in which major political events did not occur around the turning-point date.

## QUALIFICATIONS AND OBJECTIONS

We turn now to possible objections, and several necessary qualifications, to the argument advanced above. The first relates to the continuation of extreme poverty in many third-world countries. If Sri Lanka has really been developing for more than a century, how can it still rank so low in per capita income? Second, we must look briefly at the controversy over the impact of colonialism. Third, we must look into the requirements for export-led growth and why these requirements are met in some cases but not in others.

## Why Still So Poor?

The IBRD World Development Report for 1981 contains the usual listing of countries ranked by per capita income in 1979 U.S. dollars. Of these, 36 are classified as "low-income countries," with per capita incomes in the range of $100–400 per year. Twenty-one of these countries fall outside the sample taken here, usually because they do not meet the size criterion. Seven more are the countries listed earlier as not having reached the turning point. But this still leaves eight countries in our sample that, although they have passed the turning point according to my chronology, are still very poor: Burma, China, India, Indonesia, Pakistan, Sri Lanka, Tanzania, and Uganda. Half of these, to be sure, are post-1945 developers that have not had time to move far beyond their starting point. Burma and Uganda have had a disastrous recent experience after a long period of earlier growth. But a case like Sri Lanka, with an average annual per capita income of $230, is admittedly puzzling.

Certainly people in Western Europe and the United States are much better off than people in Sri Lanka, though not as much better off as the World Bank tables suggest. Simon Kuznets and more recently Irving Kravis and his colleagues on the International Comparisons Project suggest that conversion from local currencies to U.S. dollars at official exchange rates exaggerates the actual difference in consumption levels. Moreover, the degree of distortion increases with the disparity in per capita income. Adjustment to a purchasing-power basis suggests that the "official" per capita figures for the lowest-income countries should be two to three times their current levels to make them at all comparable with figures for the richest countries.

Certainly, too, per capita income in the advanced industrial countries has risen faster than it has in Sri Lanka over the past century. The income gap has been widening. But such comparisons do not bear directly on the question of what has been happening in Sri Lanka itself. Here the economic histories of the country suggest that per capita income did begin to rise significantly around 1880 and that it has risen intermittently ever since. Between 1950 and 1980, for which data are reasonably reliable, average per capita income grew at more than 2 percent per year.

The other significant development is the growing inequality of incomes that seems to characterize most, though not all, developing countries in the early stages of intensive growth. As of 1880, there was something approaching a flat plateau of poverty across the population. The increases in income since that time have been unequally distributed, and hills and valleys in the distribution have become more prominent. There may well be some Sri Lankans, especially small farmers with little marketed output, who are living today much as their forefathers lived a century ago. Those who argue that growth is illusory tend to focus on these lowest strata. But many others—sizable commercial farmers, factory workers, business and professional people, civil servants, other white-collar groups—have moved up in the income scale, while at the same time growing in relative numbers. The lower-middle and upper-middle income brackets are more thickly populated than they used to be.

In addition to higher per capita consumption of private goods and services by these groups, we should not overlook important increases in consumption of public services. Public education and public health services have been substantially strengthened in Sri Lanka, as in most other third-world countries. This must have brought some benefit to even the poorest groups in the population.

## The Question of Colonialism

We cannot enter here into a full-dress discussion of colonialism, which has its own large and controversial literature, but several comments are in order. First, we cannot safely generalize about all colonies at all times. We cannot toss all the colonial powers into one basket. Japan has always been growth-oriented, in colonial areas as well as at home; and it is clear that Japanese rule helped to initiate intensive growth in both Korea and Taiwan. In Cuba and the Philippines, intensive growth dates from transfer of the colonies from Spanish to American rule. The British were also typically growth-minded. But they tended to delegate much authority to local administrators, and so policy varied from one area to the next and even in the same colony at different times. (The case of India, which did not achieve intensive growth during the colonial era, has tended to dominate the anticolonial literature; but India is rather a special case, and most other British colonies did better.) Going downward in the scale of interest—and success—in colonial development, we may list the Germans, French, Belgians, Dutch, and Portuguese. Angola, Mozambique, and Zaire have not yet achieved intensive growth, and in Indonesia growth remains precarious. General statements professing to apply to all colonial powers and to all periods clearly cannot be true.

Second, one should distinguish several different questions that can be asked about colonial rule:

1. Did areas under colonial rule achieve a turning point and embark on intensive growth? Some did, and some did not, as is true also among countries that remained independent.
2. Could these areas have grown more rapidly had the colonial powers made indigenous economic growth a prime objective? Here the answer usually is, "Yes, more could have been done than actually was done." But here again, one must distinguish among countries and time periods. In Britain's African colonies there was a clear progression from a relative lack of interest in economic advancement of "the natives" before 1914 to a more substantial interest and even some infusion of development funds from 1920 to 1940, to strong interest in economic development and preparation for eventual independence from 1945 to 1960. For whatever reason, the two world wars were distinct punctuation marks in colonial policy.

3. Would these areas have developed more rapidly before 1950 if they had been independent countries rather than colonies? Any answer to this counterfactual question is conjectural, especially for "countries" that did not exist before colonization. But the record of countries that never fell under colonial rule— Ethiopia, Afghanistan, Nepal, pre-1949 China—is not impressive. There is no magic in independence.

Colonial rule usually made several positive contributions. It often established clear political boundaries for the first time, and experience of unified administration within these boundaries contributed to a growing sense of nationhood. Even the nationalist groups that arose in opposition to colonial rule often furnished the nucleus of later independent governments. Colonial authorities often introduced new export crops—coffee, tea, cocoa, sugar, rubber, and so on—or devised land-settlement schemes that stimulated production of traditional crops, such as rice, for export. Colonial governments usually engaged in considerable construction of physical infrastructure, notably roads, railroads, river navigation, and port facilities. Suppression of internecine warfare and maintenance of internal order were favorable to economic activity and were important in speeding population growth. Also favorable to population growth was reduction of famine through improved food transport and the spread of Western medical facilities, which became increasingly important after 1900.

There are also negative items on the scorecard. There was typically an income drain from the colony through repatriation of profits on foreign investment and in other ways. Some of the new export industries had a distinct enclave character. Even that portion of export proceeds that remained within the colony was unequally distributed within the population. The colonial authorities did little to shelter domestic handicrafts from competition from imported factory goods. They were also typically hostile to domestic industrialization, preferring continued import of manufactures from the metropolis. Education, particularly secondary and higher education, was usually undersupported. Even more serious, the colonial authorities often encouraged immigration to fill intermediate positions between the top jobs, held by Europeans, and unskilled labor, which alone was considered suitable for the "natives." This policy produced a three-tier racial division of labor, as in British East Africa or Burma, where the rulers were British, most traders, clerks, and skilled workers were Indian, while the indigenous population were farmers and laborers. Throughout Southeast Asia the Chinese filled this intermediate role, and natives of the colonies were largely walled off from occupational advancement.

The net score from adding these pluses and minuses varies from country to country, and each case must be considered on its own merits. It will be useful in this connection to look at the 41 countries in our sample. For 16 of these the colonialism issue is not relevant. Except for Cuba, the Latin American countries were not colonies after about 1820. Nine additional countries were under colonial control only briefly, or indirectly, or not at all: China, Japan, Thailand, Afghanistan, Nepal, Iran, Iraq, Turkey, and Ethiopia.

Of the countries that were colonies, 17 reached the turning point during the colonial era whereas eight did not. Those which did not include the three successor states of the Indian subcontinent—India, Pakistan, and Bangladesh—plus Indonesia, Egypt, Sudan, Mozambique, and Zaire. The fact that several very large countries appear in this group has no doubt contributed to an impression that colonial rule usually prevented economic growth, a conclusion that does not seem to be true.

All these colonies are now ex-colonies; and it is interesting to ask whether they have grown more quickly since independence than they did under colonial rule. In making such a comparison, one must recall that decolonization set in during the late 1940s and that from 1945 to 1973 world output and trade grew at an unusually fast rate. One might expect, therefore, that growth in ex-colonies would have been faster after independence than before; but this could have resulted mainly from participation in the world economic boom rather than from independence per se. Setting this point aside, and overlooking the fact that post-1950 growth estimates are somewhat firmer than those for earlier periods, a gross comparison is possible for 20 countries (four ex-colonies did not reach the turning point in either era, and Zimbabwe's independence is so recent that nothing can be said). The expectation of more rapid recent growth is confirmed for 11 of these countries. For three additional countries (Kenya, Sri Lanka, and Malaysia), the post-1950 growth rate of per capita income is not very different from that in the colonial period. This leaves six countries (Burma, Cuba, Ghana, Tanzania, Uganda, and Zambia) whose performance has deteriorated since independence, for reasons that differ in detail but can be characterized broadly as political.

The legacy of colonialism is perhaps most dubious in Africa. True, Africans in large numbers were drawn into the monetary economy, as wage earners and as producers of marketed crops. A purely arithmetical calculation shows a rise in per capita income, evidenced in larger consumption of simple consumer goods plus some improvement of public services. At the same time the racist occupational stratification that developed in most colonies was stultifying and demeaning to Africans. Public education and training of local leadership was badly neglected, which helps to explain the fragility of political systems in the postindependence period. It is no accident that the economies whose performance has deteriorated since 1960, or that have failed even to reach the turning point, are heavily concentrated in Africa.

## Stimulus to Growth from Primary Exports

In countries that reached the turning point before 1940, intensive growth was usually associated with a sharp rise in primary exports, in absolute terms and as a percentage of GDP. Exports came to be regarded as the "engine of growth." In the development literature of vintage 1950–65, however, it was fashionable to regard growth led by primary exports as unfeasible over the long run, or at any rate as inferior to other possible growth paths. The criticisms of primary exports included the following arguments: primary products are often produced by foreign-owned enterprises, with the result that much of the income flows abroad rather than stimulating the domestic economy; market prospects for primary products are poor because of low income elasticities of demand as well as material-saving technical change in the industrialized countries; because of slow growth of demand plus the difficulty of controlling supplies, terms of trade for primary products relative to manufactures are bound to deteriorate over the long run; sharp fluctuations in the value of exports, arising from wide swings in world prices as well as harvest variations, are disruptive to the economy; continued reliance on primary exports perpetuates a quasi-colonial pattern of dependence on the industrialized countries, from which an independent nation should try to break free.

The most substantial of these criticisms involves the wide swings in world prices for primary products and the consequent fluctuations in export receipts. These swings generate cycles in primary-producing countries similar to the business cycles generated by investment fluctuations in industrialized countries. But in neither case do fluctuations necessarily prevent growth, and a variety of counter-cyclical measures are available. The "dependency" argument is heavily political and, I think, somewhat superficial. Any country, including Japan and the United States, is "dependent" in the sense that its export volume is responsive to fluctuations in the world economy. But exploitation of comparative advantage and other gains from integration into the world economy more than outweighs the consequences of exposure to these fluctuations. A country can deliberately unlink itself from the world economy by trade barriers, thus achieving what is best described as isolation rather than independence; but isolation tends to lower the growth rate rather than raise it, as later chapters will make clear.

Nor have events since 1945 borne out the forecast of poor market prospects for primary products. The demand equations that Lewis fitted for the years 1886–1965 have continued to predict quite accurately. Primary exports have continued to grow at almost exactly the same rate as industrial production in the industrialized countries. Agricultural exports have grown a bit less rapidly, but mineral exports have grown more rapidly.

At any time, to be sure, a *particular* primary product may face sluggish world demand, as may be true for a particular kind of manufacture. A country practicing monoculture also faces the prospect of growing competition from other countries producing sugar, coffee, rubber, or whatever. But a country is not locked into producing any one product in perpetuity. Country economic histories reveal two interesting phenomena. The first is rotation of leadership among primary exports. At any one time a single product may bulk large in a country's export bill, but the product does not necessarily remain the same over time. Thus Argentina moved from wool to wheat to chilled meat; Mexico shifted from metals to agricultural products to petroleum; in Peru, leadership has rotated among several farm crops, several metals, and most recently a large fish meal industry.

The second important phenomenon is *diversification* of primary exports over time, meaning that instead of a single dominant export the country has a half-dozen or more important exports. Diversification does not happen in every case. Several of the oil economies have stuck with oil, copper remains dominant in Zambia and Chile, cocoa in Ghana, and sugar in Cuba. But diversification is prominent in well over half our countries and is strongly associated with export success. Especially impressive cases of primary export diversification include Brazil, Mexico, Peru, Sri Lanka, Malaysia, Thailand, Ivory Coast, Pakistan, and Indonesia.

The terms-of-trade argument has been going on for generations. Around 1900 J. M. Keynes predicted that the primary products/manufactures terms of trade must move increasingly in favor of primary products because natural resources are limited whereas manufacturing output can be multiplied indefinitely. Around 1950 Prebisch and others were predicting precisely the opposite. Most recently the ''limits of growth'' school has been predicting exhaustion of mineral resources; although these models usually employ only quantities and no prices, a rise in the relative price of minerals (and, because of the ''population bomb,'' foodstuffs as well) would logically follow.

Empirical studies by Kindleberger (1978) and others, however, fail to reveal any long-run tendency in the terms of trade. Over the past century there have been sharp fluctuations in response to boom, depression, and war. But the view that prices of primary products have undergone a secular deterioration is not sustained.

Generalized complaints about the undependability of primary exports, then, are not substantiated by the evidence. The fact remains that, from 1850 to 1914 and again from 1945 to 1973, some countries achieved substantial gains in per capita output fueled by primary exports while others did not. Exports clearly can serve as an ''engine of growth'' or at least, in Kravis's phrase, as a ''handmaiden of growth.'' But they will not always do so.

What makes the difference? Relevant factors seem to include (1) supply elasticities within the country. A sharp increase in foreign demand for a product may evoke a large supply response, or it may not. (2) The size of the export sector relative to the size of the economy will make a difference. (3) The disposition of the export proceeds—how much remains in the domestic economy to raise incomes and stimulate local demand—is clearly very important. Let us consider these points in turn.

1. As Lewis (1978b) has emphasized, the challenge of rising export opportunities must be met by an adequate production response within the country, which may or may not occur. Examination of our country cases suggests several things which influence a country's supply responsiveness:

    a. Natural-resource supplies. This is most clearly a factor for mineral expor-
       ters, but it is important also for exporters of agricultural products. For
       example, the tropical crops for which world demand was rising rapidly from
       1850 to 1914 usually required either irrigated land or land with adequate
       natural water supply. Where there was a plentiful supply of unused, well-
       watered land, as in West Africa, Ceylon, Burma, and Thailand, export
       volume could be increased rapidly by bringing more land under cultivation.
       But where virtually all the good land was already occupied, as in Egypt or
       Java, possibilities of export expansion were limited. In other cases the
       export response was sluggish because land-ownership patterns prevented
       peasant producers from getting access to land, as in the Philippines or
       Venezuela.
    b. Diversity of resources and products. It is true that Brazil rode the coffee
       wave and West Africa rode the cocoa wave for long periods of time. But
       reliance on a monoculture is precarious, partly because of the certainty of
       growing competition from other countries. Successful exporters succeed
       partly by gradual diversification of exports, which reduces the importance
       and the associated risk attaching to any one product.
    c. Government capacity and government policy. Nothing is easier than to
       prevent or stifle economic growth. A government that is unable to maintain
       internal order, that lacks minimal administrative capacity, that is so little
       interested in growth that it fails to provide the necessary physical and human
       infrastructure, or that follows trade and tax policies strongly biased against
       exports can readily prevent a country from reaching a turning point. There
       are numerous examples of success and failure in these respects among both
       colonial administrations and independent governments.
2. The relative size of the export sector is self-evidently important. A small
   engine will have difficulty moving a large train. If exports are only a few
   percent of GDP, even a high rate of export growth will mean only a small
   increase in per capita income. The size of the export sector is related partly to
   geographic size of the country and the ratio of coastline to hinterland. China,
   for example, has a huge hinterland that until recently was linked to the coast
   mainly by river transport. It is estimated that around 1900 only about 2 percent
   of China's national product entered into international trade. The trade ratio of
   India seems to have been somewhat higher but, partly because of supply and
   transport difficulties, the export growth rate from 1870 to 1914 was below that
   of most other third-world countries. So the stimulus to this large and sluggish
   economy was quite limited. Even since 1950, growth in per capita income in
   neither country can be attributed to any extent to export growth. In India, the
   export/GDP ratio *fell* considerably between 1950 and 1980, to a current level
   of only about 5 percent. China's trade ratio is also very low, though it has risen
   somewhat since 1975.

Quite different is the situation of smaller economies such as Taiwan, Thailand, Malaysia, Sri Lanka, Ivory Coast, Ghana, Peru, or Chile—not to mention Hong Kong, Singapore, and dozens of others that fall below our size limit. Here the export/GDP ratio quickly reached 20–30 percent, sometimes even 50 percent, and a substantial percentage of the population was drawn into export production. Models of export-led growth offer a good description of the experience of these countries.

3. Finally, much depends on the disposition of the export proceeds. *Returned value* to the domestic economy can be defined as net exports (value of goods sold abroad *minus* value of imported materials used as inputs) less transfers accruing to foreigners (such as repatriation of profits by foreign owners). Returned value, calculated as a percentage of net exports, is a key statistic that many authors have attempted to estimate. Its size is influenced by foreign or domestic ownership of productive assets. It is influenced also by the labor intensity of the production process and by the extent of linkages to other sectors via input purchases. Historically, foreign-owned petroleum enterprises come closest to the model of a pure economic enclave with minimum spread effects to the domestic economy. Plantation agriculture is somewhat more favorable to domestic growth. Still more favorable is small-scale peasant production of export crops.

Returned value depends also on how far government chooses to tax export income in one way or another. It is thus partly a policy variable, not just a fact of nature.

Critics of primary exports have tended to focus on the enclave cases, but these are by no means predominant. By far the most common situation, exemplified especially by West Africa and Southeast Asia (but found also in countries as diverse as Colombia, Pakistan, and Taiwan), is one in which agricultural exports come from owner-occupied farms of moderate size. The responsiveness of small farmers to income incentives has been demonstrated repeatedly. In these cases returned value is high, accruing primarily to the farmers but secondarily to government through export taxation.

Of 30 countries in our sample characterized by export-led growth, 21 depended almost entirely on agricultural exports. In 10 countries export crops were grown almost exclusively by peasant producers on small farm units. In 11 additional countries small farm units coexisted with larger commercial farms or plantations (Sri Lanka, Tanzania) or sugar estates (Philippines, Cuba).

In four countries (Indonesia, Malaysia, Peru, Mexico) agricultural exports, coming partly from small farmers, were combined with substantial mineral exports. Only five countries (Chile, Venezuela, Zambia, Iraq, Iran) were almost exclusively mineral exporters.

The most interesting feature of the mineral economies is the way in which governments gradually appropriated more of the export proceeds. To induce initial exploration and investment, the government usually offered very favorable royalty terms to private companies. Once a company had invested, however, its properties were hostage to subsequent tax increases. The company retained some leverage through its ability not to increase its investments or to curtail production and thereby reduce the country's export receipts. A threatened tax increase was often countered by an "investment strike." The dispute was eventually settled on terms involving some increase in taxation, investment was resumed, and the stage was set for the next round in the bargaining game. Thus governments that had initially received only a few percent of the rents from mineral exploitation eventually came to receive 50 percent or more. The eventual outcome was usually nationalization of company properties.

This process has been described in detail for Venezuela by Franklin Tugwell (1975), for Chile by Markos Mamalakis and Clark Reynolds (1965), for Iraq by Edith and E. F. Penrose (1978), and for Iran by Julian Bharier (1971). It scarcely corresponds to the picture sometimes presented of helpless governments subservient to foreign interests.

To sum up: although the turning point is *usually* associated with a marked rise in the export/GDP ratio, this is not an invariable rule. It has not been true in India, where the trade ratio has declined during the intensive-growth era. China has also followed a relatively autarkic, inward-looking development path. Other exceptions among recent developers include Egypt and Turkey, whose export/GDP ratios in 1978–80 were only about half as high as in 1950–52. Closed-economy models of internally generated growth would be relevant to these cases. In a large majority of cases, however, export performance is the best single clue to the initiation and continuation of intensive growth.

# 4

## The Pattern of Intensive Growth

What happens after the turning point? We are looking at 34 countries scattered over three continents and most of the earth's surface. Intensive growth in these countries began at different times, ranging from 1840 to 1965. How far can we generalize over such a broad sweep of space and time?

A number of statistical regularities have been revealed by the work of Kuznets, Chenery, and others. As per capita income rises there is a gradual shift in the composition of national output, with the agricultural sector shrinking and the industrial and service sectors growing in relative importance. A similar shift occurs in the uses of output, with a relative decline in the share of private consumption and an increase in the shares of public consumption and investment.

But when we look below these macroeconomic totals we find a great deal of variation: in the pattern of institutional change, in the pace of sectoral shifts, in the sources of increased agricultural and industrial output, in the product composition of output, in foreign trade and financial flows, in the orientation of economic policy and the frequency of policy shifts. This rich variety of country experience stands out clearly in the country case studies and can be fully appreciated only by reading them. In an effort at summation, I shall venture some generalizations that seem to hold true for most countries in the sample. But there is hardly any statement to which one cannot find exceptions, and these will be duly noted.

One interesting question relates to the difference between pre-1945 and post-1945 experience. The post-1945 era brought general decolonization, a faster tempo of world economic growth, new institutions for transfer of capital and technology, a new climate of opinion emphasizing the responsibility of government to promote economic growth. Thus late developers were arriving at the turning point under different conditions from those facing early developers; and the post-1945 growth path of the early developers was affected in important ways. At the end of this chapter I shall offer some summary comments on development then and now.

POPULATION AND LABOR SUPPLY

Even in the last century, the beginnings of intensive growth typically brought some acceleration in the rate of natural increase in population. A gradual sag in mortality rates was mainly responsible. The reasons included improved transport facilities to move food to areas that might otherwise have experienced famine; gradual spread of vaccination against infectious diseases from the late nineteenth century onward; reduction of infant mortality through improved water supply, sewer systems, and maternity clinics; growing availability of curative services by doctors and hospitals; and improvements in nutrition, education, and personal health care, all raising natural resistance to disease. Improvements in health and nutrition may also bring some increase in (unregulated) fertility rates. There are examples of rising fertility in our country cases; but on the whole fertility changes appear minor compared with the effect of declining mortality.

But while endogenous changes would have produced some acceleration of population growth in developing countries, they cannot explain anything like the rates of increase actually observed. These rates have been due mainly to discontinuous jumps in the progress of medical science, associated particularly with the two world wars and impinging on third-world countries as an exogenous factor provided virtually free of charge by international agencies. Medical progress produced a marked reduction of deathrates in the 1920s and an even more dramatic reduction after 1945; reductions occurred even in countries that have not yet reached the turning point. The average rate of population increase in third-world countries is estimated by Kuznets (in Easterlin, 1980) at only about 0.6 percent per year from 1850 to 1900. By the 1920s it had risen to 1.3 percent. By 1950–55, it had risen to 2.0 percent and by 1970–75 to 2.6 percent, as crude deathrates fell from an average of 31 per thousand in 1937 to 16 per thousand from 1970 to 1975.

This sharp acceleration of population growth has placed late-developing countries in a different position from that of their predecessors. Late developers have had to run faster to outpace population growth and achieve increases in per capita income. In general, third-world countries have responded successfully to this challenge. The rates of GDP growth achieved since 1945 would have appeared sensational in the nineteenth century. After deducting high rates of population growth, however, the growth rates of GDP per capita are only moderate. The detailed country data to be presented in chapter 15 show also that there is no significant relation between the rate of population growth and the rate of increase in per capita income, that is, countries with higher population growth have managed on average to offset this increase by faster growth of total output. This observation supports a similar conclusion reached earlier by Kuznets for the "developed" countries.

Higher rates of population growth have also altered the labor-supply situation. While "surplus labor" can be defined in a variety of ways, I take it as meaning unutilized labor time that does *not* reflect a preference for leisure but rather lack of opportunity for productive employment. In the pre-1940 era surplus labor was limited to a few densely settled areas: Egypt, Java, parts of China and India. Latin America, Africa, and even much of Asia had reserves of unused land that could readily absorb population growth. Indeed, managers of mines and plantations commonly complained of the scarcity of labor. What this often meant, however, was unwillingness to pay wages high enough to attract people from a relatively comfortable living in agriculture. It was for this reason that Brazil imported slaves and later European immigrants, that Ceylon imported Tamil laborers from southern India, that Malaya imported Chinese, and so on.

Since 1945, however, accelerated population growth has produced surplus-labor conditions in more and more countries. The effects of surplus labor are seen in underutilization of agricultural labor, excessive migration to the cities, over-crowding of "traditional" trade and service activities, and open unemployment. The pressure for employment tends also to produce compulsory overstaffing of industrial enterprises, particularly public-sector enterprises, as well as govern-ment agencies. As always, there are exceptions. A few countries with unusually high growth rates, notably Taiwan and South Korea, have exhausted the surplus-labor pool and entered the era of labor scarcity. But such situations are unusual.

It is usually thought, following the well-known Lewis model, that surplus labor is accompanied by a constant real wage rate. In some countries one does observe this, but in others one does not. Where agricultural productivity is rising, a rise in agricultural wages may put pressure on the urban wage level. Large em-ployers may voluntarily pay a premium wage in order to recruit, stabilize, and motivate an industrial labor force. It is possible also for the urban real wage level to be forced upward prematurely through political mechanisms. Unions of workers in government and large-scale industry, often concentrated in and near the capital city and often linked to political parties, are in a good position to win minimum-wage legislation and high pay scales in government, which often serves as wage leader for the economy. This premature forcing up of urban wage scales tends to restrict urban employment opportunities while at the same time increasing the incentive to rural-urban migration. It thus aggravates the problem of urban unem-ployment and underemployment.

To end this section on a more cheerful note: in the older industrial countries, after an initial spurt of population growth associated mainly with declining mor-tality, the birthrate began to follow the deathrate downward, eventually reducing population growth to a modest 1 percent or so per year. This process seems now to be setting in among third-world countries. In 15 countries in our sample, including almost all the rapidly growing countries, the rate of natural increase was *lower* in 1980 than in 1960. In some cases the decline was quite sharp: in Chile from 2.5 to 1.5 percent, in Colombia from 3.2 to 2.2 percent, in Brazil from 3.0 to 2.1 percent, in South Korea from 3.0 to 1.7 percent, in Thailand from 2.9 to 2.2 percent. All the other Latin American countries in our sample show declines, as do Malaysia, Indonesia, Taiwan, Turkey, Philippines, and Sri Lanka. Although data for China are not precise, there is no doubt that birthrates and the population growth rate have been reduced substantially by the government's active population-control program.

The reasons for declining birthrates no doubt vary from country to country and could be revealed only by careful case studies. The limited evidence suggests that, while family-planning programs have had some effect, the main factors are associated with rising per capita income and resemble those operating earlier in the "developed" countries: lower infant mortality, which reduces the number of births needed to achieve a desired family size; urbanization, which leads to a decline in birthrates because children are more expensive and less useful in cities than in the country; better education, which tends to raise people's aspirations both for themselves and their children; and especially improved education and higher socioeconomic status for women, which seems strongly associated with lower birthrates.

In regard to population, then, the normal pattern is for the growth rate to rise for a considerable time after the beginning of intensive growth. Eventually, however, developments associated with rising per capita income have a retarding influence on the birthrate. The decline in the birthrate eventually exceeds the parallel decline in the deathrate (which is still continuing even in developed countries), and the rate of natural increase begins to fall. Experience in the older industrial countries suggests an eventual leveling off of the population growth rate at something like 1 percent per year.

### AGRICULTURE AND FOOD SUPPLY

Over the course of intensive growth, while the agricultural sector is shrinking in relative terms, output is normally rising in absolute terms. Rising agricultural output serves several familiar functions. First, except for a limited number of oil-mineral economies, agriculture is initially the main source of rising exports. Some of these export crops may have been newly introduced to the economy—cocoa in West Africa, tea in Sri Lanka, rubber in Malaysia, sugar in Cuba and Philippines—but others may be traditional food crops, such as rice, which are produced in increasing volume to meet rising foreign demand. In a land-surplus situation, which has existed in most countries until quite recently, production for export is added on to domestic food production rather than displacing it.

Second, agriculture is the main, often the exclusive, source of food supply for the growing population. In a poor country with low nutritional levels, income elasticity of demand for food is quite high, perhaps in the range of 0.6–0.7. For example, if population is growing at 2 percent and per capita income is also growing at 2 percent, food demand will be rising at more than 3 percent per year. If food output rises less rapidly than demand, the internal terms of trade will turn in favor of agriculture, with upward pressure on food prices and money wage rates; this will tend to choke off industrial growth, as Ricardo predicted. The food constraint can be relaxed, of course, through food imports, but this course also has costs and risks.

Finally, a growing population needs more jobs as well as more food, and for a long time agriculture remains the main source of increased employment. True, migration to the cities sets in early. If a country's population is growing at 2 percent the rural population may be growing at only 1.5 percent. But since 80 percent of the population is rural in the first instance, the rural sector still accounts for a lot of people in absolute terms. Additional employment for them has to come from some combination of increase in cultivated acreage, application of more labor inputs per acre, and diversion of rural labor time into small-scale industry and other nonagricultural activities. In some cases—Japan after 1880, Taiwan after 1950, China after 1950—this absorption of farm-family labor time in non-farm activities has been quite important. Although densely populated China has not yet achieved full employment, a study by Rawski (1979) indicates that it was much closer to it in 1979 than in 1950.

Whereas the development literature of the 1950s emphasized industrialization as the key to progress, the recent tendency has been to place increasing emphasis on agriculture. It is now standard doctrine that agriculture plays a central role as provider of exports, foodstuffs, and employment.

When we look at production experience, however, we find some surprises. Even in the 1970s, when the "green revolution" had worked its benign effect in many areas, five of the 19 countries with highest GDP growth rates were raising food production at less than 3 percent per year. Of the 18 countries at the bottom of the growth league, 16 were raising food output at less than 3 percent. Thus more than half the countries in our sample were not meeting what could be considered a modest standard of agricultural performance.

In some cases, to be sure, there is a plausible explanation. Countries with a strong position in oil or mineral exports can trade these products for food imports, thus relaxing the pressure on food production. This would apply to such cases as Iraq, Nigeria, Egypt, Algeria, Chile, and Peru, in all of which food imports have been rising rapidly. Even so, food imports use foreign exchange that could be put to other uses. Further, any interruption of the export flow can place the country in a precarious position.

In another eight countries, per capita income growth from 1960 to 1980 was near zero or even negative. This group includes Zambia, Zaire, Nepal, Mozambique, Sudan, Uganda, Ghana, and Afghanistan. In these cases low growth in agriculture is part of a pattern of low GDP growth and, indeed, is a large component of poor overall performance. These cases provide negative confirmation of the key importance of agriculture.

The most interesting countries are those which have achieved modest growth of GDP per capita in spite of substandard agricultural performance, thus apparently contradicting the conventional wisdom. In this group are Kenya, Morocco, Tanzania, India, and Burma. These cases might be regarded as showing that strong growth of agricultural output is not *essential* for overall growth. But agricultural growth is still very *helpful*. The GDP growth rate of these countries could have been considerably higher if agricultural performance had been better.

This having been said, agricultural output normally rises during intensive growth, and in the more successful economies it rises at a good rate. For the dozen most rapidly growing countries in our sample (excluding the oil economies), the median annual growth rate of food output in the 1970s was 4.5 per cent. And even some of the oil countries did quite well, as for example Indonesia (3.6 percent), Iran (4.0 percent), and Venezuela (4.0 percent).

This leads to the next question: where do output increases come from, and why are some countries able to raise output more rapidly than others? Agricultural organization is important, with owner-operated farms clearly superior, though tenancy systems that assure security of tenure and moderate rentals can also perform well. Land reserves are always helpful, though their exploitation requires investment in infrastructure. Technical progress is always necessary and must be relied on increasingly as the frontier closes. Government can contribute in important ways: by changing agricultural organization so that more income accrues to the cultivator; by investment in irrigation and drainage, roads, warehouses, and marketing facilities; by agricultural research and extension services; and by helping to ensure adequate supplies of credit, seeds, fertilizers, and other inputs. The converse of this is that government can readily choke off agricultural growth by doing the wrong things or by sheer neglect.

The pattern of agricultural organization existing at the turning point may already be favorable to intensive growth. In quite a few Asian and African countries (Burma, Thailand, Nigeria, Ghana, Ivory Coast, Uganda) small, owner-operated farms have always predominated. Another group had a combination of small and medium-sized farms (Chile, Argentina, Brazil, Peru, Colombia, India, Pakistan). In still other cases foreign-owned plantations were established to grow export crops, while food was produced mainly by small indigenous farmers (Sri Lanka, Malaysia, Philippines, Indonesia). The least favorable situations were those in which large landowners dominated a mass of peasant cultivators (Mexico, Venezuela, Egypt, Iran) or in which European settlers had appropriated much of the best land and developed a modern agricultural economy on top of the traditional indigenous economy (Algeria, Morocco, Kenya, Zimbabwe). These last situations were unstable in the sense that they could not survive the transition to independent rule.

Where the initial situation is unfavorable, usually because of excessive landlordism, there has often been a major "land reform" early in the intensive-growth era. Land reform typically takes the form of a ceiling on landholdings, with holdings above the ceiling purchased or confiscated by government and subdivided into small farms whose new owners pay for the land over a period of years. A nominal purchase sometimes turns into a confiscation, as in cases where the large landowners are paid off in government bonds whose value later shrinks through continuing inflation. Reforms of this type, intended to provide strong incentive to small cultivators, occurred in Japan (1873), Mexico (nominally after the 1910 revolution, but implemented mainly in the 1930s and 1940s), Taiwan (1949–53), South Korea (early 1950s), Egypt (1952), Iraq (1958 and 1970), Iran (1960 and 1965), and Kenya (1960 onward). These reforms are generally judged to have made a substantial contribution to the subsequent rise in agricultural output.

A different type of reform has involved transformation of formerly private (and, in some cases, foreign-owned) holdings into cooperative or communal farms. This happened in China after 1949, Cuba after 1958, Algeria after 1962, Mozambique after 1975, and Tanzania ("villagization program" of the 1970s). The only one of these cases that can be considered moderately successful is China, where agricultural output has rather more than kept pace with population since 1950. In the other cases the results have been poor.

A word now about the input sources of output growth. In examining the literature I was surprised to find that almost every country had surplus land as of 1900 and that quite a few still had surplus land in 1950. The closing of the frontier has been very gradual. But the process is inexorable, and in one country after another the possibilities of further expansion of acreage are being exhausted. As this happens, the burden of raising agricultural output is shifted increasingly to technical progress. Generalizing for the third world as a whole, we can say that over the past century the contribution to output of increases in acreage has become steadily less important, while the contribution of higher yields per acre through technical progress has become steadily more important.

In addition to the growing importance of new technology, the nature of technical progress has changed substantially. Until recently yield increases came mainly from traditional technical progress, of the type illustrated by our discussion of China in chapter 2: modest improvement of seeds through selection and transference; irrigation and drainage to regulate water supply; larger per acre inputs of labor and organic fertilizer; shifts in the cropping pattern toward crops yielding more calories per acre; more continuous use of land, with shorter fallow periods. Since World War II, however, there has been a rapid development of modern or science-based technical progress, involving systematic and sustained research and experimentation. The Mexican center for wheat and corn research (CYMMIT) and the Philippine center for rice research (IRRI) developed new seed varieties that provided large increases in crop yields. The success of these ventures has stimulated establishment of other international centers for research on sugar, potatoes, and a variety of tropical crops.

Use of these new seeds, often called "high-yielding varieties" (HYV), typically requires a "package" of complementary inputs—water supply, chemical fertilizers, pesticides, more-intensive tillage. These must be applied in carefully regulated proportions to achieve optimal results. Further, it appears that a country cannot simply "borrow" seed varieties developed elsewhere. Considerable research and experimentation within the country is necessary to domesticate the new strains to local soil and climate conditions. Countries that have moved energetically to incorporate HYV seed into their agricultural systems have been able to achieve remarkable yield increases within a few years. The most dramatic examples come from Southeast Asia (Thailand, Burma, Taiwan, Philippines, Indonesia), but India, Pakistan, Turkey, and Egypt have also made substantial gains.

I noted above that accelerated population growth since 1945 has made the food-supply problem more urgent than before. At the same time, intensified technical progress in agriculture has provided at least a potential answer to this need. But one cannot be uniformly optimistic. There are a number of countries, particularly in sub-Saharan Africa, where yields per acre are static or even declining and where domestic food supplies are falling increasingly behind the growing population's needs.

In addition to reforming tenure systems, building rural infrastructure, and supplying modern inputs and new technology, government can influence the cash returns from farming through purchase of output by government marketing boards, farm price controls (or lack of such controls), pricing of government-supplied fertilizer and other inputs, exchange-rate policies (which determine the return from agricultural exports), and industrial-protection policies (which affect the prices farmers must pay). Harsh policies that tax farmers heavily can discourage cash-crop production and even cause a reversion to subsistence farming. A shift toward more generous policies, which a good many countries made in the 1960s and 1970s, can lead to a sharp rise in output. This point will be elaborated and illustrated in chapter 6.

THE INDUSTRIAL SECTOR

"Industry" must be viewed broadly as including household and handicraft production as well as factory output. Indeed, the early developers often had few or no factories at the turning point. For countries reaching the turning point after 1945, such as China, India, Egypt, Turkey, and Indonesia, there was already a modest development of factory industry. But even in these cases handicrafts still provided most of industrial output.

The rapid expansion of foreign trade typically associated with the turning point has two main consequences. To the extent that revenue from exports is returned to the economy, domestic demand for all goods and services, including manufactures, is increased. But tradable goods need no longer be obtained from domestic sources. Handicraft producers have to compete with imports, whose volume tends to rise in tandem with export volume. Although the *market share* of handicraft producers declines, there is not necessarily an absolute decline in output. Since total demand is rising, the volume of handicraft production may be maintained or even continue to grow slowly. Further, the impact of import competition is uneven by product and region. It is usually most severe in textile spinning, where the cost advantage of factory goods is very large, and hand spinning is often wiped out quickly. The decline of hand weaving proceeds more slowly, partly because availability of cheap machine-produced yarn helps the weavers to survive in competition. Producers of bulky products or producers located far from the seacoast get some protection from transport costs and may be little affected by imports. Handicraft producers of export specialties, such as Iranian carpets, will also continue to flourish.

As demand continues to grow and as the market is confirmed and mapped out by imports of manufactures, domestic factory production eventually makes its appearance. But this happens only with a considerable lag. Peru and Argentina had very small industrial sectors before 1930. Malaya, Thailand, and all the African countries except Southern Rhodesia and Kenya had scarcely any factory industry as late as 1940. Still, factories eventually appear and expand. Domestic industry grows mainly in response to rising demand; but it grows also by taking over an increasing share of the market from handicrafts and from imports. The progress of import substitution can be traced by looking at the percentage of, say, cotton-cloth consumption supplied by imports. This figure, typically falling over time and eventually approaching zero, appears in many countries' economic histories. It should be emphasized that import substitution is a normal process that will spread from products with small optimum scale of plant to those requiring larger scale, even in the absence of special stimulus. Substitution usually is stimulated in varying degree by protective tariffs, which, while they may be imposed mainly for revenue purposes, do raise domestic prices of manufactures above the world price, making it easier for domestic industries to survive. Industrialization has also been stimulated by special crises that reduced availability of foreign supplies. The two world wars, which sharply reduced the flow of manufactures from the industrialized countries, left a market gap that was filled in some third-world countries by rising domestic production. The collapse of primary-product prices during the Great Depression, which sharply reduced most countries' capacity to import, also led to a spurt in domestic industrialization, especially in Latin America.

Rising industrial output as a percentage of GDP is sometimes seen as a growth of "big business." But for a long time after industrialization begins, the number of really large establishments is limited. Industrial censuses usually show that the great majority of manufacturing enterprises are very small. The structure of manufacturing can properly be characterized as "dualistic." On one hand are enterprises with several hundred workers, with a relatively high capital/labor ratio, relatively high output per worker, and relatively high wage rates. On the other hand are a multitude of small shops with markedly lower capital/labor ratios, labor productivity, and wage rates. The small establishments typically provide more than half of factory employment, though because of their lower productivity they may provide only a quarter or less of factory output.

Notable too is the very gradual shrinkage of the handicraft and cottage-industry sector, which even today provides a surprising amount of employment in many third-world countries. A few examples may be worth citing. In Chile in 1970, after more than a century of intensive growth, about half of all industrial workers were in some 70,000 very small workshops, about 40 percent of which were producing clothing and shoes. In Colombia in the late 1960s, when factory employment was around 300,000, there were still an estimated 150,000–200,000 handicraft workers. These workers, however, produced only about 15 percent of manufacturing output, implying relatively low output per worker. In Nigeria in 1965, some 900,000 rural households were engaged in cottage industries. This compares with 100,000 in urban enterprises with 10 workers or less, and only 76,000 in firms employing more than 10 people. In the Philippines in 1970, handicraft and cottage industries with 1–4 workers provided an estimated 70 percent of industrial employment. In Morocco at the time of independence in 1956, the number of handicraft workers was reported as "substantially larger" than the number of factory workers. In Iran, too, handicraft workers were said to outnumber factory workers as recently as 1970.

Who were the early industrial entrepreneurs? In some countries foreign enterprise was quite important. American investment was prominent in the Philippines and Cuba after 1900. The early factories in Taiwan and Korea were Japanese-owned. The British were prominent manufacturing investors in Kenya, Nigeria, and the Rhodesias, as were the French in Algeria, Morocco, and Ivory Coast. In a larger number of cases, however, the entrepreneurs were homegrown. This was generally true in Latin America, provided we count recent immigrants as part of the local population. Immigrants from Portugal, Spain, and Italy, who often brought capital as well as business experience, played a considerable part in the industrialization of Brazil, Argentina, and Chile. Local enterprise predominated also in Southeast Asia, provided again we count people of Chinese origin as "local." Families that had migrated permanently from China were the main entrepreneurs in Malaya and Thailand as well as Singapore and Hong Kong; and they made important contributions in Taiwan, Philippines, and Indonesia. Although there was some British investment in manufacturing in India, Indian entrepreneurs predominated increasingly with the passage of time. In China, too, British and Japanese investors established some of the first textile mills, but Chinese gradually took over most of the manufacturing sector. In Pakistan, which had little industry at independence, the new manufacturing entrepreneurs were entirely local.

In the post-1945 period, most newly independent countries have been suspicious of or even hostile to foreign investment. Many foreign-owned enterprises have been partially or wholly nationalized, and indigenous businessmen have taken over increasingly. There has also been a substantial increase in government entrepreneurship, which is local by definition.

There is nothing unusual to be said about the sources of labor and capital inputs, nothing that would distinguish industrialization in third-world countries from the similar process in Europe or America. Leaving aside foreign-capital inflows, the initial domestic capital for new industries came usually from trade or agriculture. As had been true earlier in England and Western Europe, many of the early industrialists were merchants, often engaged previously in import trade. From serving the domestic market through imports, they turned rather naturally to serving it through local factories, using their accumulated capital to finance the initial construction. Wealthy landowners—the "coffee barons" of Brazil, the "sugar barons" of Peru, and so on—also turned their capital toward manufacturing when it became profitable to do so. Once established, the new industries grew in classical fashion through reinvestment of their large profits.

Labor supply, in the sense of sheer numbers, was rarely a problem. From the outset factories were able to offer wage rates well above those in agriculture and other alternative occupations and thus to attract a surplus of applicants. The difficulties were rather those of training, motivation, and supervision, which early industrialists often underestimated. Finding labor apparently cheap, they tended to use it inefficiently. Only gradually, and often under the pressure of rising wages, did they pay enough attention to personnel management to develop reasonable levels of proficiency. The much-discussed "labor problems" of industry in developing countries usually turn out on examination to be largely "management problems."

The normal sequence of products in an industrializing economy is quite predictable. Textiles are usually the leading sector, because clothing is a basic need and the domestic market is large. Further, the capacity to produce cotton and other fibers is widely distributed throughout the world, which means that domestic raw materials are usually available. In addition to an assured domestic demand for cloth—often demonstrated initially by large cloth imports—the emergence of textiles is facilitated by relatively small minimum efficient scale of plant, a well-known technology, ready availability of used as well as new textile machinery, and limited requirements of skilled labor.

Other early industries are concerned mainly with agricultural processing for home use or for export—rice milling, flour milling, sawmilling, palm-oil extraction, and so on. These are followed by the production of light consumer goods, such as shoes, clothing, beverages, leather goods, ceramics, furniture, and household utensils, as well as building materials and simple agricultural implements. As the market continues to grow, additional industries appear in a sequence charted by Walther Hoffman (1958) and Hollis Chenery (1960, 1979). "Middle industries," such as chemicals and petroleum products, appear next, followed eventually by "late" or heavy-goods industries, dominated by metals, machinery, and transport equipment.

In comparing the course of manufacturing growth since 1950 with that in earlier periods, one observes both similarities and differences. The basic sequence—textiles, other consumer goods, intermediate goods, capital and durable consumer goods—does not seem to have changed. Countries normally move through this sequence, with domestic production replacing imports at successively higher stages. But since 1950 there has been a more systematic effort to guide the process of industrial expansion, not only in late-developing countries but in third-world countries in general. In earlier periods, although there were general trade and exchange-rate policies that might help or hamper manufacturing growth, there was little effort to discriminate among branches of manufacturing. After 1950, with more activist governments and more attention to overall development planning, arose a widespread belief that some paths to expansion are preferable to others and that governments should guide the sequence as well as the overall tempo of industrialization.

Partly because of this proindustry policy bias, partly because of the increased resources made available by rapidly rising exports and foreign borrowing after 1950, the pace of movement through the sequence from handicrafts to light industry to heavy industry was considerably accelerated as compared with earlier eras. And in some countries the sequence itself was altered to the extent that heavy industry was expanded faster than would have happened without government intervention—and often faster than market size warranted. The socialist economies of Eastern Europe have sometimes been described as "prematurely heavy-industry oriented." The same could be said of a number of third-world countries.

Another characteristic of post-1950 manufacturing expansion was a marked increase in the public-sector share of assets and output. Before 1940 third-world manufacturing industries were almost entirely in private hands. Since 1950 in most countries government has not only been the main source of industrial finance, through government investment banks, commercial banks, and direct budget allocations, but has gone beyond fulfilling this role to ownership and management of manufacturing establishments. The public-sector share of manufacturing is often 20 or 25 percent and sometimes reaches 75 or 80 percent. The reasons vary from country to country: a long-standing statist tradition, as in Turkey and other remnants of the Ottoman Empire; socialist ideology of the British Labour Party type, as in India; a desire to transfer industry from foreign to national ownership, which tended to be interpreted as public ownership, as in Egypt or Burma; and a perhaps natural tendency for government investment banks to acquire majority equity ownership and thus responsibility for management, as in Mexico or Brazil.

These publicly owned manufacturing industries on the whole have not operated very efficiently, with the result that there have been recent reversals of policy in a number of countries. This range of problems will be examined further in chapter 6.

THE FOREIGN SECTOR

Since early intensive growth is normally export-led, a rising trade ratio follows almost by definition. During the 1870–1914 era, third-world countries that had entered on intensive growth typically had population growth rates of around 1 percent, GDP growth rates of 2–3 percent, but export growth rates of 3–4 percent. The export/GDP ratio was thus typically rising.

After 1945, export pessimists such as Prebisch argued that growth led by primary exports was no longer feasible. The rules of the game had changed. But the export record since 1945, presented in some detail in chapter 15, fails to confirm this gloomy prognosis. In most countries the export/GDP ratio was higher in 1980 than in 1950. Significantly, this was true especially of countries *with high growth rates*. Of the 19 countries with the highest growth of per capita income, 15 had a higher export/GDP ratio in 1980 than in 1950. Thus exports were still operating as a leading sector. Countries in which the export/GDP ratio declined are clustered toward the bottom of the growth-rate table. In India, for example, with a below-average growth of per capita output, the export/GDP ratio fell from 6.7 percent in 1950–52 to 4.9 percent in 1978–80. This decline is related to inward-looking economic policies unfavorable to exports, described more fully in later chapters. Most of the other cases are African countries, where the falling export ratio is symptomatic of political disorganization and low economic growth. Examples are Tanzania, Zambia, Uganda, Zaire, and Ghana. But in the more successful African countries, Kenya and Ivory Coast, the trade ratio has risen.

Arguments about the limited stimulating effect of primary exports often seem to assume that a country keeps on exporting the same products in perpetuity and that, if returned value to the domestic economy is initially low, it will remain low. But neither of these premises is realistic. One of the more striking features of the oil-mineral economies is the demonstrated ability of governments to extract a growing share of the export proceeds by taxation and by raising the price of labor and other domestic inputs. A few examples: in *Chile,* returned value from the copper industry rose from 38 percent in 1925 to about 80 percent by the late 1950s. In *Peru* returned value, which comes from agricultural and fishery products as well as minerals, had risen to 53 percent by 1960 and 81 percent by 1973. In *Venezuela* the government share of net income in the oil industry rose from a low initial level to 51 percent in 1950 and 80 percent in 1973. In *Iraq,* the privately owned Iraq Petroleum Company paid only a low fixed royalty; but in 1951 the government succeeded in enforcing a fifty-fifty sharing of profits, and when the oil company proved resistant to further concessions it was nationalized in 1972. In *Iran,* too, the British-owned Anglo-Iranian Oil Company paid only a meager royalty up to 1950; but when the company refused to concede a larger share, it was nationalized and the government share of oil revenue jumped sharply. In none of the countries studied has the trend been in the opposite direction.

A second striking development is that many countries, and especially the more successful exporters, have managed to diversify their export bill over time. Thus even where the export of goods that were dominant in the early days has grown slowly or even declined, the growth rate of total exports has been maintained by adding on new products. Again a few examples, drawn from our country case studies, will be helpful: in *Brazil,* where coffee, sugar, cotton, and cocoa still formed 89 percent of exports in 1960, the share of these traditional goods had fallen to 36 percent by 1976. New exports include soybeans and derivatives (17 percent), iron ore (10 percent), and manufactures (30 percent). *Mexico* in the 1870–1910 era was mainly a mineral exporter. But by the 1950s, due mainly to an active government policy of agricultural development, Mexico was exporting a diversified list of agricultural and livestock products and minerals were of minor importance. Still more recently have come oil and growing exports of manufactures, in addition to a large tourist industry. In *Ivory Coast* the "big three"— cocoa, coffee, and logs—were traditionally close to 100 percent of exports. But today these goods are exported increasingly in processed rather than raw form, and the country has added cotton, palm products, and fruit as well as growing exports of manufactures. The *Philippines* traditionally exported sugar, copra, and coconut oil, to which have now been added logs, plywood, copper concentrates, and manufactures (about 20 percent of exports.)

In *Pakistan,* raw cotton fell from 40 percent of exports in 1950 to 14 percent in 1980. Rice exports are now larger than cotton exports, and still more important are finished manufactures (42 percent) and semifinished goods (16 percent). In *Sri Lanka,* traditional tea, rubber, and coconut exports have fallen from 95 percent to 60 percent of the total. New agricultural exports, as well as manufactured exports, have been rising rapidly. In *Malaysia* tin and rubber, which were 90 percent of exports in 1950, have now fallen below 50 percent. New exports include timber, palm oil, petroleum, and manufactures. *Thailand*'s traditional export of rice, which for many decades accounted for about 70 percent of all exports, has now fallen below 20 percent. New exports include maize, kenaf, cassava, rubber, timber, and manufactures (about 22 percent of the total).

These examples make clear that many third-world countries have succeeded not only in diversifying their exports of primary products but also in penetrating the huge world market for manufactures. The most spectacular examples are South Korea and Taiwan, where manufactures now form close to 90 percent of all exports. The "gang of four," which includes these countries plus Singapore and Hong Kong, now supplies about half of all third-world exports of manufactures (a percentage that is probably at its peak and will fall as manufacturing capacity expands elsewhere). But quite a few other countries have succeeded in raising manufactures from a few percent of exports in 1950 to 20–30 percent by 1980. The list includes Mexico, Brazil, Colombia, Egypt, Turkey, Pakistan, Sri Lanka, Thailand, and Philippines.

In terms of dynamic comparative advantage, one might expect labor-intensive manufactures to migrate increasingly to third-world countries having abundant labor and relatively low wage rates. The main retarding factors are import quotas and other restrictions imposed by the developed countries, plus the time and effort needed to bring third-world industries up to a competitive level of productivity and costs. In addition to competing in developed-country markets, it should be possible for third-world countries increasingly to exchange manufactures with each other. Already a good share of manufactured exports from Brazil are to other Latin American countries, from Ivory Coast to other African countries, from Egypt and Pakistan to the Arab oil states, and so on.

Rising exports mean rising capacity to import. The import/GDP ratio tends to parallel the export/GDP ratio, rising when exports are buoyant, falling when exports are doing poorly. More interesting is the commodity composition of imports, which changes in a predictable way. In the early decades of intensive growth, consumer goods and especially textiles usually dominate the import list. But as the country develops its own light industries, consumer-goods imports decline steadily as a percentage of total imports and as a percentage of domestic supply of consumer goods. The composition of imports shifts toward capital goods, fuels, and intermediate goods needed as inputs to manufacturing. These items now dominate the import list in most third-world countries, with consumer goods only a quarter or less of all imports. The main exception is a number of countries that, as noted earlier in the chapter, have allowed food production to lag behind population growth, with the result that food imports may constitute 20 or 30 percent of the import bill.

Imports tend to run ahead of exports, the balance being closed by foreign borrowing. It is natural for a developing country to be a borrower for quite a long period. The United States, Canada, and Australia were large net borrowers during the nineteenth century, and so were several countries in Eastern Europe. This has also been the general rule in the third world, the main exception being Japan, which was unusually successful in mobilizing domestic capital and in earning foreign exchange through a rapid increase in exports. More recently, China has developed mainly from internal resources, except for substantial Soviet credits in the 1950s and a modest infusion of Western capital in the post-Mao period.

Much has been written on capital transfers from developed to developing countries. Anything that could be said within the limits of space here would have to be quite superficial, and so it is perhaps best to say nothing. The literature suggests that foreign capital, while quite helpful to some countries at some times, has rarely been critical. The key requirements for growth lie in the domestic economy and polity; and where these requirements are absent, foreign capital is unlikely to be used effectively.

I have tended in this section to view export-led growth as the standard case and to view a rising export/GDP ratio as helpful, if not essential. So it is important to note exceptions. China's trade ratio since 1950 has been low. India's trade ratio has been low and declining. A similar decline is evident in Egypt and Turkey over the 1950–80 period. It is no doubt easier for a large country, with diverse resources and a large internal market, to follow an autarkic, inward-looking development path. India and China can do things that would not be feasible for Jamaica or Gambia. Even in the Indian case, however, most economists conclude that more outward-looking policies and more concern for exports would have made possible a higher growth rate than that actually achieved.

My interpretation implies also a standard *pattern* of growth, broadly similar for most developing countries. Other writers, however, have tried to distinguish several distinct *patterns* of growth and to classify countries on the basis of which pattern they fit. Such efforts usually rely mainly on the differing behavior of the foreign sector. Thus Paauw and Fei (1973) distinguish between (1) continued reliance on growth of primary exports, (2) import-substitution policies aimed at accelerating the growth of the industrial sector, and (3) export substitution, in which manufactured goods increasingly replace primary products in the export bill.

I prefer to regard these not as *alternative* growth patterns but as successive *stages* in a historical sequence. A country begins by exporting primary products, since they are all it has. As income from exports broadens the domestic market, the industrial sector grows through the normal import-substitution sequence outlined in the previous section. This sequence can no doubt be accelerated by protectionist trade policies, but it is not clear that a specific degree of import restriction warrants placing a country in a separate category, especially in view of the variability of policy over time. Many countries that followed restrictionist policies for a decade or two after 1945 concluded eventually that continued growth of the industrial sector required development of export capacity in manufactures, aided by a more outward-looking policy stance.

A successfully developing country, then, tends to move through the three Paauw-Fei stages in sequence, ending up with a large component of manufactured exports. Taiwan and South Korea are classic examples, but a dozen other "newly industrializing countries" are now following the same trajectory. Countries differ, however, in the tempo of movement through the sequence. These differences stem partly from the richness and variety of the natural-resource base. A country with a strong resource base can afford to be more leisurely about manufacturing development, which will occur in any event unless thwarted by obtuse policies. Size of country is also a major consideration. Larger size, by providing a large domestic market, tends to hasten the rate of industrialization and broaden its pattern, so that even "late" industries arrive fairly soon.

The large country–small country dimension and the rich resources–poor resources dimension yield a four-box classification of countries that could prove useful. The growth experiences, and especially the industrialization experiences, of countries in different boxes probably do differ in a systematic way. To this extent one may be justified in speaking of *patterns* of growth.

THE PUBLIC SECTOR

Government functions as a producer of public and quasi-public goods and as an important investor in physical capital. Looking first at the former function: it is familiar knowledge that the public consumption/GDP ratio in developed countries is substantially higher today than it was fifty years ago. High income elasticity of demand for education and health services, a tendency to stretch the public-good concept to cover more and more things, and the fact that most of the cost of public goods is labor cost and so reflects wage scales that typically rise faster than prices, all contribute to this result.

In the third world, too, there is a marked difference between earlier times and the post-1945 situation. Estimates of national income before 1940 are rare; but where they have been made, it appears that public consumption was rarely more than 5 percent of GDP. Colonial governments tended to service mainly the European population, which was concentrated in urban areas. The peasant in the countryside received much less attention. Education in particular was notably underdeveloped. But one can scarcely say that independent countries were more enterprising. The Latin American countries, for example, had very small public sectors before 1940, and their public consumption/GDP ratios are still relatively low.

Since 1950 we do have national-income estimates for almost all countries and tables showing the distribution of income among private consumption, public consumption, and capital formation. A tabulation of the data for the countries in our sample appears in chapter 5. The relative importance of public output has risen substantially over time. By 1950, the median public consumption/GDP ratio for countries in our sample was already about 10 percent. By 1980 the median had risen to 13 percent. Of the 30 countries for which a comparison can be made, 26 show an increase in the ratio over this period. Although these are nominal figures, there was no doubt also a rise in the real level of public services. In most countries real per capita income was rising; and demand for education, health services, and other public goods is quite income-elastic. Further, where national governments had replaced colonial governments, these new governments were likely to be more responsive to public demands. The demonstration effect of the richer countries and the activities of international bodies such as the World Health Organization (WHO) and the United Nations Educational, Scientific, and Cultural Organization (UNESCO) must also have stimulated expansion of public output.

There is marked intercountry variation in the public output/GDP ratios. The 1980 ratios ranged all the way from 28 percent in Zambia and 22 percent in Morocco to 8 percent in Colombia, Ghana, Sri Lanka, and the Philippines. Except for Argentina, the Latin American countries have relatively low public-goods output. Other countries with low ratios include Thailand, Pakistan, Sudan, India, Sri Lanka, Ghana, and the Philippines. There is no obvious economic basis for these intercountry differences, which do not correlate closely either with 1980 per capita income levels or with 1950–80 growth rates.

The allocation of expenditures differs rather widely among countries, but a few generalizations can be made. The largest allocations are typically for defense, general administration, and education. Defense is the most variable item, taking less than 10 percent of the budget in Mexico, Colombia, Kenya, and Ivory Coast, but about 30 percent in Turkey, Thailand, and South Korea, and close to 50 percent in Taiwan, Pakistan, and Iran. General administration typically takes 10–20 percent of the budget, and the median figure for education is also around 20 percent. Large educational expenditure is explained by high population growth rates, which result in a large school-age component in the population, and by the fact that universal primary education is in most countries a high-priority objective. There is wide intercountry variation, however, with most Latin American countries unusually light on education and Philippines, Malaysia, Taiwan, and Ivory Coast unusually heavy. Health, housing, and other social services typically take 5–10 percent of the budget, and economic services something like 20 percent. This amount is usually distributed fairly equally among agriculture, roads and infrastructure, and other economic purposes, though again there is considerable intercountry variation.

Turning to government's role as investor, we again note a marked change in recent decades. We have inadequate data for the pre-1940 era, but it is estimated that gross capital formation as a percentage of GDP probably did not exceed 10 percent in most third-world countries. In Argentina, Brazil, Mexico, Taiwan, and Korea the rate may have been somewhat higher. Most investment, moreover, was private. Governments built roads and public buildings, made irrigation improvements in some countries, and sometimes contributed capital to railway construction. In many cases, however, government simply encouraged private railway companies through land grants, profit guarantees, or guarantee-of-bond issues.

Table 5 shows a large increase in the postwar period in gross capital formation rates. By 1950 the median rate for the countries in our sample was already 14 percent. By 1980, the median rate for the top half of our sample—19 countries with highest growth of per capita income—was 28 percent, though this falls to 21 percent for the next nine countries in the growth-rate ranking and to 12 percent for the nine least successful economies. These nominal gross capital formation/GDP ratios are somewhat higher than the real ratios because of the relatively high prices of capital goods in third-world countries. Even so, countries in the top half of our sample were investing, in real terms, about the same proportion of GDP as the richer industrial countries.

Government has participated heavily in, and in some countries has been largely responsible for, this upsurge of investment. Regular government departments build roads and bridges, urban streets and sewage systems, schools and hospitals, public buildings and military installations. In addition, many economic activities are organized as semiautonomous public corporations. The public sector now normally includes rail transport, electric power, and other public utilities; frequently includes mining and some branches of manufacturing; and sometimes extends to banking and trading activites. These corporations also have substantial investment programs, which are included in measuring the percentage of total gross domestic capital formation (GDCF) accounted for by public-sector capital formation (PSCF).

For the mixed economies in our sample (that is, excluding Cuba and China), the PSCF/GDCF ratio is usually in the range of 30–50 percent. Countries toward the lower end of the range are of two sorts: (1) Latin American countries that are already quite industrialized and have a vigorous private sector—thus the PSCF/GDCF ratio is about 30 percent in Colombia and Mexico and about 35 percent in Brazil: and (2) other countries with a strong private-enterprise orientation, such as South Korea and Thailand, where the ratio is also about 30 percent. Countries at the high end of the range include Turkey (50 percent), which has a strong statist tradition and many public manufacturing corporations; Ivory Coast (50 percent), which is still in the stage of infrastructure building; pre-1979 Iran (60 percent), where the large oil revenues flow in the first instance into government channels; and India (more than 60 percent), which has a large public manufacturing sector.

This prominence of government as investor is not new. The conventional picture of early European and American growth as a private, capitalist development overlooks the importance of government in organizing, helping to finance, and (in most countries) eventually owning railway systems and other forms of infrastructure. True, the PSCF/GDCF ratio for early developers was low by modern standards, usually in the range of 10–20 percent. But in two countries, Japan and Australia, it was substantially higher, rising at times to almost half of total investment. Moreover, in most of the presently developed countries, the PSCF/GDCF ratio has risen over the course of time. For 15 of these countries, which I analyzed in a previous study,* the ratio is now typically in the range of 30–40 percent.

The fact remains that, in third-world countries today, the PSCF/GDCF ratio is substantially above what it was in the richer countries *at a comparable stage of development*. One reason is the extension of the concept of the public sector to include not only public utilities but parts of mining, manufacturing, and other economic activities.

The large increase in government spending on current services and on investment implies a corresponding increase in government revenues. Space does not permit an extended discussion of revenue performance. Briefly, the current revenue/GDP ratio has risen substantially in most countries since 1945. By 1980 the median ratio for countries in our sample was almost 20 percent, though there is the same intercountry variation observed on the expenditure side. Revenues have been increased partly by considerable diversification of tax structures, with the share of revenue coming from a fall in import and export taxes and a rise in the share of taxes on income and wealth.

In only a few cases—South Korea, Taiwan, Brazil—is government revenue sufficient to cover both current and capital expenditures. A sizable public-sector deficit is the general rule. Part of the deficit can usually be covered by domestic

---

*Lloyd G. Reynolds, "Public Sector Saving and Capital Formation," *Government and Economic Development*, ed. Gustav Ranis (New Haven: Yale University Press, 1971), pp. 516–51.

nonbank borrowing, the feasibility of which depends on private saving propensities, on the existence of financial institutions for transfer of savings, and on offering savers an adequate real rate of return. Foreign borrowing contributes in greater or lesser degree. The last resort is central-bank borrowing, which beyond a certain point generates inflationary pressure. Country experience in this respect varies widely. The more successful economies typically use bank financing only moderately and show marked price stability. Heavy reliance on banks and high inflation rates are most common among countries that are relatively poor, that are growing slowly or not at all, and that show poor economic management by government.

THE BEHAVIOR OF TOTAL OUTPUT

Can we say anything, after this sector-by-sector review, about the typical behavior of GDP in the course of intensive growth? Not very much. We have estimates only for the post-1950 period, which for most countries is a small part of the intensive-growth era. So we are forced to surmise about what the figures for earlier periods would look like if they were available. I surmise that this hypothetical record would broadly resemble that which Kuznets has compiled for the developed countries from about 1860 onward. Specifically:

1. There is an initial period, which can be as long as two or three decades, during which the growth rate of per capita output rises from near zero to some "normal" level, that is, normal for the particular country and for the era in question. For countries whose intensive growth began before 1914, "normal" might have meant 2 percent per year (roughly the average rate for the Kuznets countries). For countries whose intensive growth began after 1945, 3–4 percent per year is normal.

   This initial increase is typically associated with export behavior. The export sector usually grows at a considerably faster rate than does GDP, which means that the export/GDP ratio is rising. The high growth rate of the export sector, plus its growing weight in the economy, gradually pulls up the overall GDP growth rate. But because of supply constraints, and occasionally because of demand constraints as well, the export/GDP ratio does not continue to rise indefinitely. As it levels off, the GDP growth rate also tends to level off at a normal or characteristic rate for the country, but a rate that varies among countries.

   This mechanism of export-propelled, or at least export-lubricated, growth seems to have operated since 1945 in much the same way as before 1945. India and China, however, stand out as notable exceptions in the recent period.

2. When I speak of a "normal" growth rate for a country, I do not mean one that is stable or invariant. Just as in the developed countries, third-world growth rates have been responsive to long swings in the world economy. Countries that embarked on intensive growth before 1914 and that had attained growth rates normal for that era grew less rapidly in the years 1914–45 as developed-

country growth slowed down. After 1945 growth rates rose again, and in most countries they were higher than ever before. There are also marked short-term fluctuations in growth rates, associated mainly with fluctuations in primary-product prices and export proceeds, that resulted partly from economic fluctuations in the developed countries affecting their demand for primary products. The most dramatic of these was the 1929–33 downswing, but the recent 1979–82 downswing was also substantial.

3. In any era one chooses, growth rates differ substantially among third-world countries. This is readily documented for recent decades. Growth rates of real GNP per capita from 1960 to 1980 range from 7.0 in South Korea to 0.2 in Zambia and −1.0 in Ghana. To explain these intercountry differences is perhaps the most challenging problem in growth analysis. We shall explore this problem further in chapter 15.

   Such characteristic differerces in national growth rates appear also in the countries studied by Kuznets. For many decades Japan and Sweden have had relatively high growth rates, while Britain has stood near the bottom of the league.

4. Although the picture of a growth rate rising initially and then "settling down" at a characteristic level fits most countries, it does not fit every country. There are cases in which a country's growth rate has *accelerated* over the course of time, to a degree greater than can be explained by world economic fluctuations. The most famous example is Japan, for which case Ohkawa and Rosovsky coined the term *growth acceleration*. The two Japanese offshoots, Taiwan and South Korea, have followed a similar path. Their recent growth rates, like that of Japan, have been much above those of other apparently comparable countries. Mexico and Brazil might also be added to this list.

   There is at least one notable case of growth *deceleration*. Argentina's growth rate was highest before 1914, dropped off sharply from 1914 to 45, and has continued at a subnormal level in recent decades. Rated as comparable with Canada and Australia in 1914, Argentina has now fallen far behind these countries and may soon drop below Brazil. There are also a few cases of *reverse development,* in which per capita income was rising for a long period but has recently gone into decline. In Uganda during the Amin regime of 1971–79, the processes regarded as characteristic of development went into reverse: people moved back from the monetary economy to the subsistence economy, monetized output dropped sharply, investment and exports almost disappeared. A similar process of undevelopment, on a less dramatic scale, seems to be under way in Ghana.

## THE DISTRIBUTION OF INCOME

Thus far I have detoured around issues of income distribution, partly because of the complexity of these issues, partly because of limited information for most countries. But there is some relevant literature, which justifies a brief comment.

In thinking about income distribution in a third-world country, it is useful to decompose it into: (1) distribution among rural households, which still predominate greatly in most countries; (2) distribution among urban households; and (3) the urban-rural gap, which is typically large. For countries with a system of sample surveys, (1) and (2) can be measured by Gini coefficients for the rural and urban sectors and (3) is measured by the difference in median household income in the two sectors. Each of the three measures has a different set of determinants, and the three will not necessarily move in the same direction—that is, toward an increase or reduction of inequality—over the course of time.

Kuznets advanced a well-known hypothesis that inequality of personal incomes tends to increase in the early stages of economic growth. A possible explanation might run in terms of the Lewis model, in which business profits swell the number of high-income recipients while surplus labor retards the advance of real wages. But eventually, Kuznets thought and Lewis would probably agree, as full utilization of labor is approached, real wages are bid up and profit margins shrink, the process goes into reverse, and inequality begins to decrease. The Gini coefficient of household incomes thus traces an inverse U-shape, first rising (greater inequality) but reaching a peak and then falling continuously. Kuznets was able to document the second phase of falling inequality quite satisfactorily for the developed countries. The phase of growing inequality is plausible but harder to document because the data diminish in quantity and quality as we go back in time.

The Kuznets hypothesis seems also to hold for most third-world countries, though I shall note some interesting exceptions. In considering typical developments during the early decades of intensive growth, it will be useful to decompose the story into the three components distinguished above.

In the rural sector, the most important determinant of income is the distribution of property ownership. Labor being relatively abundant and land and capital relatively scarce, the property share of agricultural income is higher than in the developed countries. In a study of Colombia, Berry and Urrutia (1976) found that 62 percent of farm income was attributable to land and capital (including the human capital of farm operators) and that the "pure labor share" was only 38 percent. Moreover, land and capital ownership is highly skewed and accounts for most of the income of the top income recipients. Even the labor share is somewhat skewed by unequal division of land because, as farm size decreases, family members are able to work fewer hours per year on the farm. Thus, even if the hourly return to labor were equal across farm sizes, the small farmer would earn less.

Where land distribution is quite unequal, income inequality may grow over time because the larger farmers absorb technical progress faster than the smaller farmers. Larger incomes make it easier to finance purchases of fertilizer, improved seed, and other modern inputs. Larger farmers also tend to dominate the boards responsible for allocating farm credit and input supplies and are able to place themselves at the head of the queue. In the Philippines, for example, an employment mission from the International Labour Organization (Ranis, 1973) found clear indications of growing inequality in the rural sector. Between 1956 and 1971 the Gini coefficient for rural households rose from 0.38 to 0.46. The authors of the ILO report surmised that large farmers were adopting new agricultural technology and raising crop yields faster than were smaller farmers. Regionally, too, the poorest agricultural regions have had the lowest rate of increase in median income. There is similar evidence from India, Pakistan, Mexico, and a number of other countries.

In Taiwan, South Korea, and Thailand, on the other hand, the distribution of rural income is considerably more equal. Thailand has always been a land of small farmers, without great disparity in farm sizes. Taiwan and South Korea undertook land reforms in the 1950s that established small, owner-occupied farms as the dominant mode of production. A land-reform program usually brings a one-time shift toward greater equality of rural incomes.

In the urban sector the distribution of income, and changes in this distribution over time, depend mainly on: (1) the labor and property shares of income in the private business sector, which usually shifts in favor of profits in the early decades of growth; (2) the gap between wage levels for jobs in "modern" industry and government and the earnings of self-employed workers in traditional trade, handicraft, and service activities (Again, this gap is likely to grow in the first instance, as wages in the modern sector rise in response to rising productivity and political pressures, while earnings in self-employment are held back by the competition of migrants from the countryside.); and (3) the growth rate of modern employment, absolutely and as a percentage of the urban labor force. In a few countries, notably Taiwan and South Korea, this growth has been fast enough to exhaust surplus labor in the economy, producing a more rapid rise of real wages in both industry and agriculture and a consequent shift toward income equality.

The size of the rural-urban gap depends on developments in each sector and is influenced to some extent by government policy. In the 1950s and 1960s many third-world governments severely restrained prices paid to farmers in order to ensure cheap food for urban consumers and substantial profits for government marketing boards. This widening of the urban-rural gap both discouraged farm production and stimulated cityward migration. On the other hand, policies that pay farmers close to world prices and that, by stimulating technical progress, raise crop yields and farm incomes will tend to stabilize the urban-rural gap or even reduce it. The level of modern-sector wages in urban areas is also partly a policy variable. Where the urban wage level is pushed upward prematurely, even with large amounts of surplus labor, the urban-rural gap will widen.

Although one can find reasons for supposing that the gap will usually widen in the early period, evidence is scanty and somewhat mixed. Moreover, this evidence relates almost entirely to years since 1950, which for countries where intensive growth began before 1914 is a rather late stage. In Malaysia, Snodgrass (1980) found that the ratio of median urban to median rural household income rose from 1.84 in 1957–58 to 2.24 in 1976. The Philippines study, on the other hand, reported a modest narrowing of the gap from 2.45 in 1956 to 2.08 in 1971.

I have perhaps said enough to suggest that the overall distribution of income in a country results from a complex interplay of forces. Although forces making for growing inequality may still dominate in most countries, this is not invariably the case. It may be useful to add a word on Taiwan, where income distribution is about as equal as in the United States, and on China, where greater equality has been a high-priority policy objective.

The extent of income equalization in Taiwan, and the reasons for it, is documented in an interesting study by Fei, Ranis, and Kuo (1979). Income from agriculture was equalized considerably by the land-reform program. Important also was the policy of decentralized industrialization, which enabled a growing number of farm family members to find wage employment in nearby industries. The percentage of rural income derived from nonagricultural employment rose steeply, until by 1972 it slightly exceeded income derived from agriculture. Moreover, this rural nonagricultural activity is highly labor intensive. Since such wage income is more equally distributed than income from property or agriculture, its growing importance has reduced the rural Gini coefficient.

In urban areas the wage share of income has risen moderately and, in addition, both wage income and property income have become somewhat more equally distributed. These trends are related to the rapid growth of labor-intensive industrial exports, plus the subsequent shift from a labor-surplus to a labor-scarce economy and the resulting rapid rise in real wages. Another unusual feature of the Taiwan case is the smallness of the urban-rural income gap, which is only about 15 percent. The overall Gini coefficient for household incomes in 1972 was 0.29, placing Taiwan clearly in the "developed-country" range.

In China, there was a one-time shift toward greater equality in the 1950s. In the countryside, rich landowners disappeared and income differences based on land ownership were eliminated. In the cities, property income and private business income disappeared, and the new salary scales for managers and officials provided lower salary premiums than had existed previously. China succeeded also in establishing a poverty floor through rationing of certain necessities—grain, cooking oil, cotton cloth—and through free or heavily subsidized provision of health facilities, education, urban housing, and urban transport. This minimum standard of living is low, but the extreme poverty that one sees in many other Asian countries has been eliminated. China, it has been said, has succeeded in cutting off the two tails of the usual income distribution.

It is not clear, however, that there has been much further movement toward equality since the 1950s. Rural income differences are still wide, depending mainly on agricultural productivity in various regions. Dwight Perkins (in Dernberger, 1980) has estimated that the six richest agricultural counties in the country have a per capita income six times as high as that in the six poorest counties. Urban income differences are smaller and the urban wage-salary structure has remained relatively stable, though there is a slight tendency for the lowest wage rates to increase faster than higher rates. The urban-rural gap seems to have diminished somewhat, mainly due to government price policies favorable to agriculture. An IBRD study estimated that the ratio of urban to rural household incomes in the late 1970s was 1.7. This is not much different from ratios reported for a number of other Asian countries: Bangladesh, 1.5; India, 1.8; Sri Lanka, 1.7; Indonesia, 2.1; Philippines, 2.1; Malaysia, 2.2.

## DEVELOPMENT THEN AND NOW

I return now to a question raised at the outset: how far has the pattern of intensive growth in third-world economies since 1945 differed from that observed before 1945?

There are obviously similarities and differences. On the side of similarity: most (not all) countries conform to something like a standard pattern of intensive growth, and this seems to have been true in recent decades as in earlier decades. This pattern can be summarized as follows: the rate of population growth accelerating for a long time, but eventually peaking and then tending to decline; food output keeping reasonably apace with population growth before 1940, but falling behind in perhaps half our sample countries during the recent decades of high population growth; increases in agricultural output depending increasingly on technical progress as land availability decreases; manufacturing output rising faster than agricultural output, with a gradual shift toward larger-sized establishments and heavier types of industry, but with handicrafts and small-scale industry remaining important for a long time; the export/GDP ratio rising steeply (again, with exceptions) and then stabilizing at a rather high level appropriate to the still small (economic) size of most third-world economies; the export menu increasingly diversified, and moving eventually into significant exports of manufactures; imports running ahead of exports, implying some dependence on foreign borrowing; government playing an increasingly important role as producer of public goods, property owner, and investor, especially in the post-1945 era; the growth rate of GDP and GDP per capita rising for some time and then stabilizing at a "characteristic" level, which differs considerably among countries, and which is subject to both long swings and short-term fluctuations; increasing inequality in household income distribution, though again with important exceptions. A few countries, which have grown rapidly enough to exhaust the surplus-labor pool and enter the era of labor scarcity, have experienced an accelerated increase in the average level of real wages and sometimes also a reduction of wage differentials among occupational groups, both of which tend to equalize the household distribution.

So what is new since 1945? The impression that things are different now arises partly, I think, from the faster tempo of world economic growth in the 1945–73 period, in which most third-world countries participated. Many of the sequences of change—for example, the sequence from handicraft production to light industry to heavy industry—that were observed in the early developers from 1850 to 1914 are still observed in the 1945–80 era. But the movie projector has been speeded up, as it were, and structural change has proceeded at a faster rate than before.

But this is not the whole story. There have been additional changes, partly political and intellectual in character, but with economic consequences. Three in particular deserve comment.

1. The achievement of national independence by over half the countries in our sample had several consequences. Even where self-government came peacefully, and still more where it was achieved by military struggle, there was a natural desire to break with the colonial past, to achieve economic as well as political independence. This tended to import to economic policy a bias against trade and primary exports and in favor of industrialization in the immediate postindependence period. Further, since much of the economy had previously been under foreign control while government was now under national control, there was a tendency to identify assertion of sovereignty with transfer of economic activity to government hands. The alternative of transferring economic enterprises from foreign to domestic private owners was often not seriously considered. The relative expansion of the public sector in many ex-colonies since 1950 has more to do with nationalism than with socialist ideology, though the latter sometimes came in as reinforcement. Finally, the new national governments, even where dictatorial in character, were more responsive to popular pressure than the previous colonial administrations had been. This shows up in rapid expansion of health services, education, and other public services; in price controls and subsidization for the benefit of urban consumers; and often in forcing up of wage levels in government and industry.

2. A new climate of opinion took hold, a conventional wisdom of economic development whose main features were outlined in chapter 1. The influence of this structure of thought probably peaked around 1960, after which it was undermined increasingly by continuing research and by the record of economic success or failure in particular countries. But meanwhile it had given a special twist to economic policy in many countries: high growth targets and large five-year plans for economic development, designed partly to prove the essentiality of large-scale foreign aid; a distrust of markets and private initiative and a preference for detailed government regulation; a mystique of industrialization and a tendency to premature development of heavy industry; a tendency to regard agriculture as a resource reservoir that could be relied on to supply food and labor to urban activities, but without active measures to stimulate production; protectionist trade policies and overvalued exchange rates, which worked against exports and encouraged indiscriminate import substitution.

3. A new combination of forces impinged on third-world countries from the

developed world: advances in medical science, which for the time being led to much higher rates of population growth; advances in agricultural technology and new international organizations for disseminating this technology throughout the world; continued reduction of transport and communications costs; new channels for government-to-government transfers of long-term capital; and perhaps most important, a higher tempo of economic growth in the developed countries, which raised demand for primary products much faster than had seemed possible around 1950. On the whole, the world situation was more favorable to intensive growth in third-world countries than it had been before 1940; and even countries that made policy errors were able to do moderately well. The data in the next chapter will show, however, that some countries took much better advantage of this favorable environment than did others, while some failed to progress at all.

# 5

## Comparative Growth Performance, 1950–1980

In earlier chapters our actors were brought on stage: countries whose intensive growth began as early as 1850 in some cases, as recently as 1950 in others, plus some countries that have not yet reached the turning point. I want now to look at these countries together over the period 1950–80, because for this period we have a richer store of quantitative data. Statistics have been collected for many countries on a somewhat comparable basis by the United Nations and its specialized agencies, the IBRD, the IMF, and other international organizations. Despite some defects in measurement, these data provide a firmer empirical base than exists for any earlier period.

On the basis of this material I will comment on, and suggest answers to, some of the "big questions" about recent growth performance. For example: (1) Is recent performance related to the *time* at which a country entered on intensive growth? Do early starters have an advantage? (2) Is population a drag? Is the rate of increase in per capita income inversely related to the rate of population growth? (3) Are there other quantitative variables that may help to "explain," in a statistical sense, the intercountry variation in 1950–80 growth rates? Candidates here include country size, initial income level in 1950, export performance since 1950, agricultural performance since 1950, the investment/GDP ratio and its rate of increase over time. In addition to such economic variables, I shall explore the possible significance of political variables.

AGGREGATE MEASURES OF GROWTH

Data Problems

Information about national output and its composition comes from national accounts prepared by statistical agencies in each country. In the late 1940s the Statistics Division of the United Nations began to send an annual questionnaire to each member government, requesting national account estimates in a standard format and supposedly using standard definitions and procedures. The returns are published each year in the *United Nations Yearbook of National Accounts Statistics*. The United Nations staff is forbidden by protocol from revising the estimates of its sovereign members, so these are published essentially as submitted. The IBRD and IMF are less subject to political constraints and devote considerable staff time to revising and reestimating the country data. Wherever possible, then, I shall use IBRD or IMF sources, which reflect careful professional screening.

Revision at higher levels, however, can never fully repair inadequacies in the original estimates. Discussion with professionals in the field suggests that the estimates for countries in our sample differ widely in quality—that is, in the probable error in the estimates of major GNP components and hence, except in the unlikely event of offsetting errors, in GNP itself. For only about half the countries in our sample can the national accounts data be regarded as solid. The accounts of a few, including India, Sri Lanka, and pre-1978 Iran, approach in accuracy those of the OECD countries. Another dozen countries, including most of those with a strong growth record since 1950, show a wider but still moderate margin of error. But below this group are ten countries whose accounts are dubious, with wide error margins, and another ten for which the official data are essentially worthless. As might be expected, there is a marked correlation between poor statistics and poor economic performance. Of the ten countries with poorest data, six are on our list of countries that have not yet reached the turning point.

Especially serious is the problem of deflating money values to measure changes in real GNP. Price indexes in most of these countries do not approach the accuracy of those in the OECD countries. This imprecision is especially serious in countries with a high inflation rate. Argentina, for example, has recently had very high inflation, which has reduced the accuracy of its real product estimates. One finds countries that deflate money GDP by the consumer price index in the capital city or whose price indexes are based on a "market basket" as ancient as 1940.

So there is considerable inaccuracy in the data used here, its degree varying from country to country. There is absolutely nothing I can do about this, but it clearly complicates the problem of trying to explain differences in reported national growth rates. Part of what I will be "explaining" is differing degrees of statistical error rather than differences in economic performance.

In addition, Simon Kuznets has noted that there are several sources of upward bias in GNP estimates for third-world countries.* If we follow Kuznets, the rates reported in table 2 should be adjusted downward by at least one percentage point to make them at all comparable with rates for the developed countries. There is less distortion, however, in comparisons *within* the third-world group.

## The Reported Growth of Output per Capita

Discussions of national output used to focus on gross national product. More recently, the World Bank and others have tended to focus on gross domestic

*Simon Kuznets, "Problems in Comparing Recent Growth Rates for Developed and Less Developed Countries," *Economic Development and Cultural Change,* 20 (January 1972):185–209.

product. GDP, which measures what is produced within a country's borders, is the better measure of growth in productive capacity. GNP, which measures how much of what is produced *belongs* to residents of the country, is more closely related to changes in welfare. The distinction is not very important for the "developed" countries; but it sometimes is important in third-world countries, where an appreciable percentage of what is produced may go to foreign suppliers of capital or labor.

Further, one can look at total output or at output per capita. The latter figure will typically run 2–3 percent below the former, since 1950–80 population growth rates for the countries in our sample were typically in this range. To conserve space, I omit any tabulation of total output growth rates and go directly to output per capita.

Two somewhat different measures are presented in table 2. The first column shows average annual growth rates of GNP per capita from 1960 to 1980. I rely most on these figures because they are World Bank estimates, which have undergone the scrutiny and revision noted earlier; because data for the 1960s and 1970s are better on average than those for the 1950s, when statistical staffs had less experience and expertise; and because these are the figures recent writers on comparative growth experience have usually tried to explain.

The remaining columns show growth rates of real GDP by decade plus, in the final column, a simple average of the three decade rates. The decade rates are of interest, since they enable us to sort out countries whose performance improved steadily over the period as against those whose performance deteriorated. The figures in the last column, of course, are not "true" growth rates. A little thought will show that, if we start from a country's real per capita output in 1950 and 1980 and calculate the geometric rate of increase over this period, we will *not* arrive at the same figure as the three-decade average. But the latter figure will usually not be very different from the former, and it provides a rough indicator of performance.

In all the tables in this chapter countries are ranked in order of 1960–80 growth in GNP per capita. A ranking based on the figures in the last column would have been somewhat different, but not greatly different. The reader will note that the tables contain only 37 of the 41 countries in our sample. Omission of Bangladesh is explained by the fact that it came into existence only in 1970. In Cuba the revolution brought substantial change in statistical concepts and measurements, so that pre-1958 and post-1958 data are not readily comparable. China was not included in United Nations and World Bank tables until the mid-1970s, and even now it would be difficult to fill in a "China line" for all the later tables in this chapter. Japan is omitted because by this period it had already passed out of the "less-developed" category.

The first impression one gets from table 2 is the wide variation in country growth rates, from countries at the top, which are in the "Japan range," down to those at the bottom having negative growth rates. For convenience in later analysis, I have divided the countries into four tiers: a top group of ten countries and

TABLE 2    Selected Measures of Output Growth (percent per year)

| Country | Real GNP Per Capita 1960–80 | Real GDP Per Capita | | | Average of Decade Rates |
|---|---|---|---|---|---|
| | | 1950–60 | 1960–70 | 1970–80 | |
| South Korea | 7.0 | 2.0[1] | 6.4 | 7.5 | 5.3 |
| Taiwan | 7.1[3] | 4.0 | 6.4 | | |
| Iraq | 5.3[2] | 3.2[1] | 2.4 | 5.5 | 3.7 |
| Brazil | 5.1 | 3.6 | 2.3 | 5.4 | 3.8 |
| Thailand | 4.7 | 3.3 | 5.1 | 4.2 | 4.2 |
| Malaysia | 4.3 | 1.1 | 3.0 | 5.7 | 3.3 |
| Nigeria | 4.1 | 2.1 | 1.5 | 4.3 | 2.6 |
| Indonesia | 4.0 | 1.7 | 0.8 | 5.1 | 2.8 |
| Turkey | 3.6 | 2.9 | 3.4 | 3.2 | 3.2 |
| Egypt | 3.4 | 2.9 | 1.9 | 3.8 | 2.9 |
| Iran | n.a. | 3.3 | 6.7 | −0.1 | 3.3 |
| Algeria | 3.2 | 6.0 | −1.0 | 4.9 | 3.3 |
| Colombia | 3.0 | 1.5 | 1.9 | 3.3 | 2.3 |
| Pakistan | 2.8 | 0.4 | 3.3 | 1.9 | 1.9 |
| Philippines | 2.8 | 3.3 | 1.9 | 3.2 | 2.8 |
| Kenya | 2.7 | 1.1 | 4.6 | 0.7 | 2.1 |
| Mexico | 2.6 | 2.8 | 3.9 | 1.9 | 2.9 |
| Venezuela | 2.6 | 3.5 | 2.3 | 1.6 | 2.5 |
| Ivory Coast | 2.5 | 1.5 | 2.6 | 2.9 | 2.3 |
| Morocco | 2.5 | −0.8 | 1.2 | 2.8 | 1.1 |
| Sri Lanka | 2.4 | 1.0 | 2.5 | 3.1 | 2.2 |
| Argentina | 2.2 | 1.2 | 2.8 | 1.0 | 1.7 |
| Tanzania | 1.9 | 1.4 | 5.0 | 2.0 | 2.8 |
| Chile | 1.6 | 1.2 | 2.2 | 0.8 | 1.4 |
| India | 1.4 | 1.9 | 1.2 | 1.3 | 1.5 |
| Ethiopia | 1.4 | 2.1 | 1.9 | −0.6 | 1.1 |
| Burma | 1.2 | 4.4 | 0.2 | 1.6 | 2.1 |
| Peru | 1.1 | 2.9 | 1.9 | 0.4 | 1.7 |
| Zimbabwe | 0.7 | 2.9 | −0.6 | −2.0 | 0.1 |
| Zambia | 0.2 | 3.3[2] | 5.3 | −2.6 | 2.0 |
| Zaire | 0.2 | 2.1 | 0.5 | −2.6 | 0.0 |
| Nepal | 0.2 | 1.0 | 0.2 | 0.2 | 0.5 |
| Mozambique | −0.1 | 1.8 | 1.4 | −0.3 | 1.3 |
| Sudan | −0.2 | 2.0[2] | 0.2 | 1.2 | 1.1 |
| Uganda | −0.7 | 0.4 | 1.5 | −3.4 | −0.5 |
| Ghana | −1.0 | 2.4 | 0.0 | −2.1 | 0.1 |
| Afghanistan | n.a. | 0.4 | 0.2 | 0.2 | 0.3 |

(continued)

[1]1953–60    [2]1955–60    [3]1960–77

SOURCES: Column 1: IBRD, World Development Report, 1982. Columns 2–5: UNCTAD, Handbook of International Trade and Development Statistics, 1960–81; Taiwan [Republic of China], National Income Accounts, 1981.

TABLE 2    (*continued*)

| Country | Real GNP Per Capita 1960–80 | Real GDP Per Capita | | | Average of Decade Rates |
|---------|------|-------|-------|-------|------|
| | | *1950–60* | *1960–70* | *1970–80* | |
| Medians | | | | | |
| Tier 1 | 4.5 | 2.9 | 2.7 | 5.3 | 3.5 |
| Tier 2 | 2.8 | 2.8 | 2.6 | 1.9 | 2.7 |
| Tier 3 | 1.6 | 1.4 | 1.9 | 1.3 | 1.7 |
| Tier 4 | 0.0 | 2.0 | 0.2 | −2.0 | 0.3 |

three lower groups of nine countries each. Although the decline in per capita GNP growth rates from top to bottom is continuous and the dividing lines are in this sense arbitrary, I feel it will be useful to divide the sample into *high-growth economies* (median growth rate, 4.5 percent per year), *moderate-growth economies* (median growth rate, 2.8 percent), *low-growth economies* (median growth rate, 1.6 percent), and *no-growth economies* (median growth rate, 0.0 percent). In all tables of this chapter, countries shall be listed in this same order and median values* computed for each tier so as to enable us to form a quick impression of substantial differences in behavior.

Note that three of the top ten countries and three of the next nine are "oil economies," which benefited from the oil price explosion of the 1970s. Without oil these countries would have ranked considerably lower. The ranking of Mexico and Ivory Coast, on the other hand, appears lower than it "should" be. These are very successful economies that have a high rate of GNP growth. But population growth has also been unusually high, due in Mexico to natural increase and in Ivory Coast to substantial in-migration from neighboring African countries, which has pulled down their ranking in per capita terms.

The middle three columns of table 2 show what was happening to each country decade by decade. In about half the cases, the decade growth rates fluctuate with no marked trend. A half-dozen countries show steady acceleration, with a growth rate for the 1970s much above that for the 1950s. This group includes South Korea, Taiwan, Malaysia, Colombia, Morocco, and Sri Lanka. But there are more cases of deceleration, with the growth rate falling decade by decade. This is true of all nine countries in the lowest group, which indeed is why they ended up in this group. It is true also of Burma, Ethiopia, Peru, and Venezuela.

The medians at the bottom of the decade columns indicate that the dispersion of country growth rates widened over time, and particularly during the 1970s. In the 1950s the median growth rate for countries in tier 1, 2.9 percent, was not

---

*Occasionally a figure is available for a country in, say, 1980 but not in earlier periods. In such cases the country is excluded from the median calculation in both periods.

strikingly above that for countries in tier 4, 2.0 percent. By the 1960s, however, the gap had widened to 2.7 percent *versus* 0.2 percent; and in the 1970s tier 1 countries grew at a remarkable 5.3 percent, while those in tier 4 had negative growth of −2.0 percent per year.

This observation underlines a point made earlier. The most significant development since 1945 is *not* a widening of the average gap between third-world and OECD countries. Some widening seems to have occurred, but more significant is the sharp pulling apart of growth rates *within* the third world itself. As of the 1980s we find a top group of countries that will certainly continue to grow and (probably) to overtake the OECD countries. At the bottom is a group of stagnating or declining economies that are falling farther and farther behind the world average.

## Selected Physical Indicators

Suppose that GNP estimates were unavailable. We might then try to judge changes in per capita income by looking at physical indicators of consumption. This is useful in any event as a cross-check on GNP estimates, which as already indicated have a substantial probable error. From the many measures available, I have selected for inclusion in table 3 an indicator of nutrition (calories per capita per day), of education (primary-school enrollment as a percentage of the primary-age population), and of health (life expectancy at birth).

We cannot assume, of course, that measurement of these variables is precise. Calorie availability estimates rest on a prior estimate of food production, with adjustment for exports and imports, and are reduced to a per capita basis by dividing by the estimated population. The meaning of "primary-school enrollment" is unclear. Who is counted: those who show up on the first day? Those who show up at some point in the year? Those who are there at the end? Some fuzziness is evident when we find, as we do find in table 3, that more than 100 percent of the available children are "enrolled." Life expectancy at birth is derived indirectly from mortality rates, with changes in infant mortality having greatest influence on the result.

Look first at food availability. In anything pertaining to agriculture, three-year averages are usually used to even out the effect of harvest fluctuations. And because data for the 1950s are not very complete or reliable, we are limited to the short period from the mid-1960s to 1980. As of the base period 1964–66, 25 of our 37 countries fell within the narrow range of 2,000–2,250 calories per day, though there were extreme values such as Argentina's 3,241 and Indonesia's 1,750. The striking fact, however, is that there was little relation between a country's growth-rate ranking and its nutrition level. The median for tier 4 is only 100 calories below that for tier 1. We must of course bear in mind that calorie *requirements* vary among countries, for climatic and other reasons. Even if all populations were adequately nourished, we would find considerable variation in caloric intake per capita.

TABLE 3    Changes in Welfare: Some Physical Indicators

| Country | Food Availability (per capita calories per day) | | | Primary-School Enrollment (percent of age group) | | | Life Expectancy at Birth (years) | | |
|---|---|---|---|---|---|---|---|---|---|
| | 1964–66 | 1978–80 | Change | 1950 | 1980 | Change | 1960 | 1980 | Change |
| South Korea | 2,100[2] | 2,946 | +846 | 53 | 109 | + 56 | 54 | 65 | +11 |
| Taiwan | 2,008[1] | 2,824 | +816 | 48 | 99 | + 51 | 63 | 72 | + 9 |
| Iraq | 2,050 | 2,643 | +593 | 16 | 116 | +100 | 46 | 56 | +10 |
| Brazil | 2,460[1] | 2,517 | + 57 | 28 | 93[5] | + 65 | 57 | 63 | + 6 |
| Thailand | 2,220 | 2,301 | + 81 | 52 | 96 | + 44 | 51 | 63 | +12 |
| Malaysia | 2,430 | 2,650 | +220 | 45 | 92 | + 47 | 57 | 64 | + 7 |
| Nigeria | 2,160 | 2,335 | +175 | 16 | 98[5] | + 82 | 39 | 49 | +10 |
| Indonesia | 1,750 | 2,295 | +545 | 29 | 112 | + 83 | 41 | 53 | +12 |
| Turkey | 2,760 | 2,965 | +205 | 50 | 101 | + 51 | 51 | 62 | +11 |
| Egypt | 2,605 | 2,949[1] | +344 | 26 | 76 | + 50 | 46 | 57 | +11 |
| Iran | 2,030 | 2,912 | +882 | 16 | 101[3] | + 85 | 46 | 59 | +13 |
| Algeria | 1,890 | 2,406 | +516 | 15 | 95 | + 80 | 47 | 56 | + 9 |
| Colombia | 2,190 | 2,255 | + 35 | 28 | 128 | +100 | 53 | 63 | +10 |
| Pakistan | 1,838 | 2,300[1] | +462 | 16 | 57[5] | + 41 | 44 | 50 | + 6 |
| Philippines | 1,900 | 2,315[1] | +415 | 74 | 110 | + 26 | 51 | 64 | +13 |
| Kenya | 2,240 | 2,055 | −185 | 26 | 108[5] | + 82 | 47 | 55 | + 8 |
| Mexico | 2,568[1] | 2,803 | +243 | 39 | 120 | + 81 | 58 | 65 | + 7 |
| Venezuela | 2,221[1] | 2,649 | +428 | 40 | 104[5] | + 64 | 58 | 67 | + 9 |
| Ivory Coast | 2,430 | 2,623 | +193 | 4 | 76[5] | + 72 | 37 | 47 | +10 |
| Morocco | 2,130 | 2,651 | +321 | 11 | 76 | + 65 | 47 | 56 | + 9 |
| Sri Lanka | 2,186[1] | 2,249 | + 63 | 54 | 100 | + 46 | 62 | 66 | + 4 |
| Argentina | 3,241[1] | 3,386 | +145 | 66 | 112[5] | + 46 | 65 | 70 | + 5 |
| Tanzania | 2,140 | 2,025 | −115 | 10 | 104 | + 94 | 42 | 52 | +10 |
| Chile | 2,520 | 2,732 | +212 | 66 | 117 | + 51 | 57 | 67 | +10 |
| India | 2,051[1] | 1,998 | − 53 | 21 | 76[4] | + 55 | 43 | 52 | + 9 |
| Ethiopia | 2,150 | 1,729 | −421 | 3 | 43 | + 46 | 36 | 40 | + 4 |
| Burma | 2,010 | 2,286 | +276 | 9 | 84[3] | + 75 | 43 | 54 | +11 |
| Peru | 2,256[1] | 2,166 | − 90 | 43 | 112[5] | + 69 | 48 | 58 | +10 |
| Zimbabwe | 2,550 | 1,911 | −639 | 44 | 88 | + 44 | 45 | 55 | +10 |
| Zambia | 2,250 | 1,982 | −258 | 35 | 95[5] | + 60 | 40 | 49 | + 9 |
| Zaire | 2,040 | 2,133 | + 93 | 33 | 90[4] | + 57 | 40 | 47 | + 7 |
| Nepal | 2,030 | 1,914 | −116 | 3 | 91 | + 88 | 37 | 44 | + 7 |
| Mozambique | 2,130 | 1,891 | −239 | 12 | 93 | + 81 | 37 | 47 | +10 |
| Sudan | 2,090 | 2,371 | +281 | 6 | 51 | + 45 | 39 | 46 | + 7 |
| Uganda | 2,029 | 2,016 | − 13 | 18 | 50[5] | + 32 | 44 | 54 | +10 |
| Ghana | 2,160[1] | 1,862 | −298 | 19 | 69[5] | + 50 | 40 | 49 | + 9 |
| Afghanistan | 2,060 | 1,833 | −227 | 3 | 30[5] | + 27 | 34 | 37 | + 3 |

[1]1961–65    [2]1962    [3]1977    [4]1978    [5]1979                    (continued)

SOURCES: Food availability, FAO, *Production Yearbook*, 1960–82. Primary-school enrollment: UNESCO, *Statistical Yearbook*, 1963, 1982. Life expectancy: UN, *Demographic Yearbook*, 1960–82; IBRD, *World Tables*, 1980; and IBRD, *World Development Report*, 1982.

TABLE 3   (*continued*)

| Country | Food Availability (per capita calories per day) | | | Primary-School Enrollment (percent of age group) | | | Life Expectancy at Birth (years) | | |
|---|---|---|---|---|---|---|---|---|---|
| | *1964–66* | *1978–80* | *Change* | *1950* | *1980* | *Change* | *1960* | *1980* | *Change* |
| **Medians** | | | | | | | | | |
| Tier 1 | 2,190 | 2,647 | +459 | 37 | 99 | + 62 | 51 | 63 | +12 |
| Tier 2 | 2,190 | 2,406 | +226 | 26 | 80 | + 54 | 47 | 59 | +12 |
| Tier 3 | 2,168 | 2,249 | + 83 | 21 | 100 | + 79 | 47 | 56 | + 9 |
| Tier 4 | 2,090 | 1,914 | −176 | 18 | 88 | + 70 | 40 | 47 | + 7 |

Over the ensuing fifteen years, most countries show a marked improvement in food availability, and this is strongly correlated with the reported growth rate. In tier 1 countries, median food availability rose by 459 calories; but in tier 4 countries it *fell* by 176 calories. Every country in tier 1 and all but one in tier 2 show an increase in food availability; but seven of the nine countries in tier 4 show a decline. This suggests that the GNP estimates on which our country ranking is based did distinguish rather successfully between fast-growing, slow-growing, and deteriorating economies.

The findings for education and health are somewhat different. As of 1950, the tier 1 countries already had a primary-school enrollment ratio about double that of the tier 4 countries. But it is striking that, over the next thirty years, almost every country brought its enrollment ratio close to the 100 percent* mark. Since the tier 4 countries were lower to begin with, they actually improved *more* than the tier 1 countries over these thirty years. The reality is no doubt less rosy than the statistics suggest. The bare numbers tell us nothing about quality of instruction, length of attendance during the school year, numbers of repeaters, or how many reach a grade 4 or grade 8 level of competence. Still, the impression remains that, even in countries with low or zero growth rates, governments have been under pressure to mount crash programs of primary education and have been able to find funds for these programs.

In regard to life expectancy, too, it is striking that every country in the table shows substantial improvement, ranging for most countries from 7 to 12 years. Here, however, there is some relation between a country's reported growth rate and the degree of health improvement. The median increase in life expectancy is 12 years for tier 1 and tier 2 countries, but only 9 years for tier 3 and 7 years for tier 4 countries.

*A figure *above* 100 percent may indicate a substantial number of repeaters—students above normal primary-school age but still in the primary grades. Or it may simply reflect misreporting.

Table 3 does not reveal many anomalies—that is, cases in which the story told by GNP measures conflicts sharply with that told by physical indicators. Brazil, with a high growth rate, shows little improvement in calorie availability and substandard performance on life expectancy. In Kenya, with a superior growth rate, calorie availability has actually declined. Farther down the table, Burma and Sudan have done *better* on physical indicators than their low growth rate suggests. In general, however, the physical data do not overturn the rankings based on GNP estimates.

Table 3 does suggest that, in drawing conclusions about changes in per capita consumption or welfare, it is important to distinguish among different elements in consumption. It is apparently quite possible for educational opportunities, health facilities, and perhaps other items of public consumption to improve even in an economy whose overall growth rate is low or negative. This serves as some offset to the decline in food availability and perhaps in other items of private consumption.

CHANGES IN THE COMPOSITION OF OUTPUT

From the work of Kuznets and others it is well established that growth of national output is accompanied by systematic changes in the composition of output. Since the data are readily available, it seems worthwhile to present them.

## Output by Sector of Origin

The standard sectoral division of output distinguishes (1) agriculture, forestry, and fisheries; (2) industry, including mining, manufacturing, public utilities, and construction; and (3) services, including government, trade, finance, professional and personal services. In addition to showing these major divisions in table 4, I have separated out the manufacturing component of industry.

The agricultural data are well behaved. Agriculture is expected to shrink in relative importance, and it does shrink. Moreover, the rate of shrinkage is directly related to the rate of economic growth. Over the years 1950–80, the median agriculture/GDP ratio for tier 1 countries was cut in half, while for tier 4 countries it fell considerably less. As of 1980, then, agriculture averaged only 21 percent of GDP in the tier 1 countries but was still 41 percent in tier 4 countries. There are a few high-growth countries, including Malaysia and Ivory Coast, in which agriculture has shrunk less than would be expected. This reflects the strong agricultural base of these countries and the importance their governments attach to agricultural development. There are several low-growth countries—Burma, Uganda, Zambia—in which the share of agriculture has *risen*, contrary to expectations. This typically reflects disorganization of the money economy and a reversion to subsistence agriculture.

The figures for industry are somewhat distorted by inclusion of mineral and oil production, which accounts for the very high 1980 figures for industry in the oil-exporting countries. If we allow for this distortion, the industry figures behave as expected. The industry sector grows in relative importance, and its rate of expansion is directly related to the rate of economic growth. Consequently, by 1980 industry contributed almost twice as much to GDP for tier 1 countries as did agriculture. In tier 4 countries the reverse was true. Again, there are cases in which the industry percentage *fell* between 1950 and 1980. These cases reflect special circumstances, such as the decline of the copper industry in Zambia and general economic disorganization in Uganda and Zaire.

Looking more narrowly at manufacturing, we note first that several Latin American countries were already quite industrialized in 1950. In Argentina, Brazil, Chile, and Mexico, manufacturing already contributed more than 20 percent of GDP. For other parts of the third world, however, this was not true. The typical manufacturing/GDP ratio was only about 10 percent, and for most tier 4 countries it was even lower.

The next thirty years saw a marked relative expansion of manufacturing. By 1980 a dozen countries had manufacturing/GDP ratios above 20 percent, including not only the spectacular cases of Taiwan and South Korea but also Thailand, Malaysia, Egypt, Turkey, Colombia, Peru, and the Philippines. The rate of manufacturing expansion is clearly related to the rate of economic growth. By 1980 the median manufacturing/GDP ratio had reached 22 percent for tier 1 countries, but it was still only 6 percent for tier 4 countries.

This association does not mean that more rapid industrialization was the *cause* of more rapid GNP growth. As I argued in chapter 4, manufacturing growth is more properly regarded as an accompaniment or even a consequence of overall growth. The dominant influence was expansion of consumer incomes and domestic demand fueled by export expansion, which in the 1950s and 1960s was mainly expansion of primary exports. In addition, factory industry gradually won a larger share of the market by displacing both imported manufactures and domestic handicraft production. The widespread prevalence of government policies favoring industrialization was no doubt helpful. But the influence of policy is often overemphasized relative to the autonomous response to market growth.

The "services" sector is very heterogeneous, and to say much about it would require subdividing it into major types of service—such as trade, government output, personal services—and looking separately at each.

## Consumption, Investment, Government

We turn now to the division among private consumption, public consumption, and investment (see table 5). This is a distribution not of domestic output but of

TABLE 4  Output by Sector of Origin (percent of GDP)

| Country | Agriculture | | | Industry | | | Manufacturing | | | Services | | |
|---|---|---|---|---|---|---|---|---|---|---|---|---|
| | 1950 | 1980 | Percent Change | 1950 | 1980 | Percent Change | 1950 | 1980 | Percent Change | 1950 | 1980 | Percent Change |
| South Korea | 47² | 16 | − 66 | 15 | 41 | +179 | 10 | 28 | +183 | 38 | 43 | + 12 |
| Taiwan | 19 | 9 | −111 | 24 | 46 | + 92 | 17 | 43 | +153 | 57 | 39 | − 32 |
| Iraq | 22 | 7 | − 68 | 50 | 73 | + 45 | 6 | 6 | 0 | 28 | 19 | − 31 |
| Brazil | 27 | 10 | − 63 | 24 | 37 | + 57 | 21 | 23 | + 10 | 52 | 53 | + 2 |
| Thailand | 58 | 25 | − 57 | 16 | 29 | + 81 | 10 | 20 | +100 | 26 | 46 | + 76 |
| Malaysia | 37⁴ | 24 | − 35 | 18 | 37 | +106 | 9 | 23 | +156 | 45 | 39 | − 13 |
| Nigeria | 67 | 20 | − 70 | 6 | 42 | +556 | 3 | 6 | +100 | 27 | 38 | + 41 |
| Indonesia | 51³ | 26 | − 49 | 17 | 42 | +154 | 12 | 9 | − 25 | 32 | 32 | 0 |
| Turkey | 49 | 23 | − 53 | 16 | 30 | + 88 | 11 | 21 | + 91 | 35 | 47 | + 35 |
| Egypt | 35² | 23⁵ | − 35 | 15 | 35 | +137 | 11 | 28 | +146 | 50 | 42 | − 16 |
| Iran | 29⁴ | 9⁶ | − 69 | 33 | 52 | + 37 | 11 | 12 | + 9 | 38 | 35 | − 8 |
| Algeria | 33 | 6 | − 82 | 24 | 57 | +139 | 13 | 14 | + 8 | 44 | 37 | − 15 |
| Colombia | 39 | 28 | − 27 | 22 | 30 | + 39 | 16 | 22 | + 35 | 40 | 42 | + 5 |
| Pakistan | 56 | 31 | − 47 | 8 | 25 | +198 | 7 | 16 | +129 | 33 | 44 | + 35 |
| Philippines | 39 | 23 | − 42 | 20 | 37 | + 82 | 12 | 26 | +111 | 40 | 40 | 0 |
| Kenya | 38² | 34⁵ | − 11 | 21 | 21 | 0 | 10 | 13 | + 35 | 41 | 45 | + 9 |
| Mexico | 20 | 10 | − 51 | 31 | 38 | + 21 | 22 | 24 | + 8 | 48 | 52 | + 8 |
| Venezuela | 8 | 6 | − 25 | 47 | 47 | 0 | 10 | 16 | + 60 | 45 | 47 | + 4 |
| Ivory Coast | 43⁴ | 34⁵ | − 21 | 14 | 22 | + 57 | 7 | 11 | + 57 | 43 | 44 | + 2 |
| Morocco | 30¹ | 18 | − 40 | 25 | 32 | + 30 | 10 | 17 | + 72 | 46 | 50 | + 9 |
| Sri Lanka | 56 | 28 | − 50 | 10 | 30 | +216 | 4 | 18 | +414 | 35 | 42 | + 20 |
| Argentina | 14² | 12 | − 14 | 38 | 41 | + 8 | 29 | 33 | + 14 | 48 | 39 | − 19 |
| Tanzania | 63 | 54⁵ | − 14 | 16 | 13 | − 18 | 6 | 9 | + 50 | 22 | 33 | + 54 |
| Chile | 14 | 7 | − 50 | 37 | 37 | 0 | 24 | 21 | − 12 | 50 | 56 | + 13 |
| India | 50 | 37 | − 26 | 16 | 26 | + 63 | 11 | 18 | + 61 | 34 | 37 | + 9 |

| | | | | | | | | | | | |
|---|---|---|---|---|---|---|---|---|---|---|---|
| Ethiopia | 65[4] | 51 | − 22 | 12 | 16 | + 33 | 11 | 11 | 0 | 23 | 33 | + 44 |
| Burma | 38 | 46 | + 20 | 7 | 13 | + 97 | 5 | 10 | +100 | 50 | 41 | − 18 |
| Peru | 35 | 8 | − 77 | 24 | 45 | + 88 | 15 | 27 | + 82 | 41 | 47 | + 15 |
| Zimbabwe | 18[4] | 12[5] | − 33 | 35 | 39 | + 11 | 17 | 25 | + 47 | 47 | 49 | + 4 |
| Zambia | 9[2] | 15 | + 61 | 71 | 39 | − 45 | 3 | 17 | +400 | 19 | 46 | +138 |
| Zaire | 34 | 32[5] | − 6 | 28 | 23 | − 19 | 5 | 4 | − 23 | 38 | 45 | + 19 |
| Nepal | 69[7] | 57 | − 17 | 10 | 13 | + 30 | 8 | 4 | − 50 | 21 | 30 | + 43 |
| Mozambique | | | | | | | | | | | | |
| Sudan | 61 | 38 | − 38 | 11 | 14 | + 32 | 4 | 6 | + 50 | 29 | 48 | + 68 |
| Uganda | 67[2] | 76 | + 14 | 12 | 6 | − 50 | 8 | 6 | − 25 | 21 | 18 | − 14 |
| Ghana | | | | | | | | | | | | |
| Afghanistan | 58[4] | 48[6] | − 17 | 10 | 12 | + 20 | 9 | 9 | 0 | 30 | 32 | + 7 |
| Medians | | | | | | | | | | | | |
| Tier 1 | 42 | 21 | − 50 | 16.5 | 39 | +237 | 10.5 | 22 | +210 | 36.5 | 40.5 | + 11 |
| Tier 2 | 38 | 23 | − 40 | 22 | 37 | +168 | 11 | 16 | +145 | 41 | 44 | + 7 |
| Tier 3 | 38 | 28 | − 26 | 16 | 30 | +187 | 11 | 18 | +164 | 41 | 42 | + 2 |
| Tier 4 | 58 | 41 | − 29 | 12 | 19 | + 58 | 8 | 6 | − 25 | 29 | 42 | + 45 |

[1] 1952
[2] 1955
[3] 1958
[4] 1960
[5] estimated
[6] 1977
[7] 1966

*Note*: References in the agriculture column apply to other sectors as well. Industry includes mining, manufacturing, construction, and electricity. Services includes transport, trade, public administration, and other services.

SOURCES: IBRD, *World Tables, 1971*; IBRD, *World Development Report, 1982*.

TABLE 5  Output by End Uses (percent of GDP)

| Country | Gross Domestic Investment 1951–60 | 1980 | Percent Change | Public Consumption 1951–60 | 1980 | Percent Change | Private Consumption 1951–60 | 1980 | Percent Change | Resource Balance 1951–60 | 1980 |
|---|---|---|---|---|---|---|---|---|---|---|---|
| South Korea | 13[2] | 31 | +148 | 11 | 13 | +18 | 85 | 64 | -25 | -9 | -8 |
| Taiwan | 16 | 31 | +94 | 19 | 16 | -16 | 71 | | | -6 | |
| Iraq | 18[2] | 33 | +79 | 15 | * | | 50 | 41* | | +16 | +26 |
| Brazil | 17 | 22[5] | +29 | 13 | 14 | +8 | 71 | 67 | -6 | -1 | -2 |
| Thailand | 14 | 27 | +93 | 10 | 12 | +15 | 77 | 66 | -15 | -2 | -5 |
| Malaysia | 12[3] | 29 | +136 | 14 | 17 | +25 | 61 | 51 | -16 | +13 | +3 |
| Nigeria | 10 | 24 | +147 | 5 | 10 | +104 | 86 | 62 | -28 | -1 | +4 |
| Indonesia | 7 | 22 | +201 | 9 | 13 | +41 | 83 | 57 | -31 | +1 | +8 |
| Turkey | 14 | 27 | +90 | 14 | 13 | -7 | 73 | 69 | -6 | -2 | -9 |
| Egypt | 13 | 31 | +135 | 17 | 19 | +11 | 68 | 65 | -5 | +2 | -5 |
| Iran | 4 | | | | | | | | | | |
| Algeria | 24 | 41 | +70 | 25 | 14 | -44 | 65 | 44 | -32 | +14 | +1 |
| Colombia | 18 | 25 | +41 | 6 | 8 | +29 | 75 | 67 | -11 | +1 | 0 |
| Pakistan | 12[4] | 18 | +50 | 11 | 11 | 0 | 84 | 83 | -1 | -7 | -13 |
| Philippines | 13 | 30 | +140 | 7 | 8 | +8 | 81 | 67 | -17 | -1 | -5 |
| Kenya | 20[4] | 22[5] | +10 | 11 | 20 | +82 | 72 | 65 | -10 | -3 | -7 |
| Mexico | 17 | 28 | -61 | 5 | 12 | +131 | 79 | 62 | -21 | -1 | -2 |
| Venezuela | 26 | 25 | -5 | 13 | 13 | +2 | 53 | 55 | +5 | +9 | +7 |
| Ivory Coast | 15[4] | 28 | +87 | 10 | 18 | +80 | 73 | 59 | -19 | -5 | -5 |
| Morocco | 14[1] | 21 | +53 | 11 | 22 | +104 | 79 | 67 | -16 | -4 | -10 |
| Sri Lanka | 14 | 36 | +157 | 11 | 8 | -30 | 72 | 78 | +8 | +2 | -22 |
| Argentina | | | | | | | | | | | |
| Tanzania | 14[4] | 22 | +57 | 9 | 14 | +56 | 72 | 78 | +8 | +5 | -14 |
| Chile | 16 | 18 | +15 | 10 | 12 | +17 | 74 | 72 | -3 | 0 | -2 |
| India | 13 | 23 | +84 | 7 | 10 | +52 | 83 | 70 | -15 | -2 | -3 |

| | | | | | | | | | | | |
|---|---|---|---|---|---|---|---|---|---|---|---|
| Ethiopia | 12 | 10 | − 17 | 8 | 15 | + 88 | 81 | 80 | − 1 | − 1 | − 5 |
| Burma | 19 | 24 | − 26 | 11 | * | | 70 | 82* | | 0 | − 6 |
| Peru | 24 | 16 | − 33 | 8 | 13 | + 55 | 70 | 68 | − 3 | − 3 | + 3 |
| Zimbabwe | 30 | 18 | − 41 | 10 | 21 | +106 | 69 | 63 | − 9 | −10 | − 2 |
| Zambia | 26 | 23 | − 11 | 9 | 28 | +229 | 48 | 54 | +13 | 18 | − 5 |
| Zaire | 25 | 11 | − 57 | 13 | 12 | − 9 | 58 | 75 | +29 | + 3 | + 2 |
| Nepal | 9[4] | 14 | + 56 | * | * | | 96 | 93 | | − 5 | − 7 |
| Mozambique | 8[2] | 10 | + 24 | 11 | 15 | + 43 | 82 | 85 | + 4 | − 1 | −10 |
| Sudan | 10 | 12 | + 24 | 8 | 12 | − 56 | 82 | 85 | + 4 | + 1 | − 9 |
| Uganda | 11[4] | 3 | − 73 | 9 | 11 | + 22 | 75 | 87 | | + 5 | − 1 |
| Ghana | 15 | 5 | − 66 | 8 | 9 | + 18 | 75 | 86 | +14 | + 2 | 0 |
| Afghanistan | 17 | 14 | − 16 | 6 | 6 | 0 | 86 | 83 | − 3 | − 9 | − 3 |
| Medians | | | | | | | | | | | |
| Tier 1 | 13.5 | 28 | +108 | 13 | 13 | − 0 | 75 | 64.5 | −14 | − 1 | − 2 |
| Tier 2 | 17 | 28 | + 65 | 10 | 12.5 | + 25 | 74 | 64 | −14 | − 1 | − 3.5 |
| Tier 3 | 14 | 21 | + 50 | 9 | 13 | + 44 | 74 | 72 | − 3 | − 0.5 | − 5.5 |
| Tier 4 | 15 | 12 | − 20 | 9 | 12 | + 33 | 75 | 84 | +12 | + 1 | − 2.5 |

*public consumption included in private consumption
[1] 1952–60
[2] 1953–60
[3] 1955–60
[4] 1960
[5] estimated

*Note:* References in the gross domestic investment columns apply to other columns as well.

SOURCES: IBRD, *World Tables, 1971*; IBRD, *World Development Report*, 1982.

domestic availabilities. If imports exceed exports, as is usually the case, avail-abilities will exceed output and the three figures will add to more than 100 percent. The discrepancy is shown in the resource balance (exports minus imports) column at the right of the table.

An additional point is of some importance. The percentage distribution in table 5 reflects nominal (money) values of output. But to discover how well this method reflects the distribution of real resources we must adjust for biases in the pricing system. This is especially necessary for cross-country comparisons, be-cause the price biases are correlated with a country's income level. The prices of investment goods in less-developed countries are high relative to prices of the same goods in industrialized countries, and the discrepancy is greatest for the poorest countries. With regard to government output, on the other hand, the bias is in the other direction. The cost of producing public goods is mainly labor cost; and so a poor country with low wage rates is devoting more resources to public output than the money distribution suggests.

This question has been investigated by the International Comparison Project, sponsored by the Statistical Office of the United Nations. A recent publication* gives the following results for the ratios of *real* to *nominal* income shares for 119 countries:

| Country Group | Consumption Ratios | | Investment Ratios | | Government Ratios | |
|---|---|---|---|---|---|---|
| | 1950 | 1975 | 1950 | 1975 | 1950 | 1975 |
| Low Income | 0.942 | 0.940 | 0.905 | 0.814 | 2.057 | 1.434 |
| Middle Income | 0.949 | 0.968 | 0.955 | 0.925 | 1.769 | 1.351 |
| Industrialized | 0.951 | 1.007 | 1.060 | 1.113 | 1.161 | 0.862 |

These figures mean that the nominal ratios shown in table 5 *overstate* the real resources devoted to investment and *understate* the resources devoted to govern-ment output, the discrepancy being greatest for the lowest-income countries. Over the twenty-five years covered by the study the discrepancy decreased for the government share but increased substantially for the investment share. Thus for any comparison with ratios for the industrialized countries, which is bound to be in the back of our minds, the nominal investment ratio for low-income countries must be *reduced* substantially, whereas the nominal government share must be *raised* even more substantially.

In the industrialized countries analyzed by Kuznets, the private-consumption share of GDP has tended to fall over the long run, while the other two shares have risen. What does table 5 tell us about trends in third-world countries? Looking first at the gross-investment share of GDP, we see that in the 1950s it tended to run

*Robert Summers, Irving B. Kravis, and Alan Heston, "International Comparison of Real Product and Its Composition: 1950–77," *Review of Income and Wealth*, Ser. 26, no. 1 (March 1980):19–66.

between 13 and 17 percent. Some of the oil-mineral economies were above 20 percent, while a few economic laggards were at 10 percent or less. The interesting thing, however, is that there seems to be no significant relation between a country's investment ratio in the 1950s and its subsequent output growth. The median ratios for the four tiers in the table are not very different.

By 1980 the investment rates for the top three tiers in our sample had increased substantially. The median rate for tier 1 countries more than doubled, the tier 2 median rose 65 percent, and the tier 3 median rose 50 percent. For the unsuccessful economies in tier 4, on the other hand, the median investment rate *fell* from 15 to 12 percent of GDP. The investment rates achieved by the more successful countries are impressive. Even with the downward adjustment suggested earlier, the medians for tier 1 and tier 2 countries would remain above 20 percent, which is in line with medians for the OECD countries.

There does seem, then, to be an association between a country's *growth rate* and the *rate of increase* in its investment ratio. But this observation does not reveal the direction of causation. One could reason that the tier 1 and tier 2 countries, having achieved success in production for a complex of reasons, then had a larger surplus available for investment. Certainly this was true for the oil economies. Their revenues increased sharply, not because of investment, but through the exercise of market power. These revenues, flowing mainly through government channels, made possible a sharp increase in capital expenditure. Conversely, the tier 4 countries, with static or declining per capita incomes, could spare little for investment and did invest little. But low investment was not the *reason* for economic stagnation or decline, which usually had political roots.

The public consumption/GDP ratios in table 5 appear low; but remember the price distortion problem noted earlier. For proper comparison with the industrialized countries, a 13 percent ratio in the table should be adjusted to something like 20 percent. This is still below the developed-country median, but not so far below.

In the case of investment we saw that ratios that were initially rather uniform had by 1980 become unequal. For public-consumption ratios, the behavior is just the reverse, moving from marked disparity in the 1950s to substantial uniformity by 1980. As of the 1950s the median public-consumption ratio for tier 1 countries was 50 percent higher than those for tier 3 and tier 4 countries. But by 1980, the medians for the four tiers are almost identical.

One implication of these results is that the more successful countries exercised restraint in expanding their public sectors. In few cases did the public-consumption ratio rise by more than two or three points, and in several cases it declined. With total output rising rapidly, of course, public services could also be expanded quite rapidly *without* much increase in tax/GDP or current expenditure/GDP ratios. We can speculate that restraint in raising these ratios may have had something to do with these countries' economic success.

The tier 4 countries were in a different situation. They were under the same pressure as other countries to expand primary education, improve health facilities, and provide urban amenities. Popular demand for these public goods is strong and bears little relation to economic resources. Recall the substantial improvement in education and health facilities shown in table 3 by countries at all income levels. In countries with slow or zero growth in GDP, providing these services required raising the government *share* of GDP, often quite substantially.

It is worth noting that the public-consumption figures show only current output of public goods. They do *not* indicate the size of total government revenue or expenditure. These figures have also been rising. IBRD data show that for the middle-income economies central-government revenue as a percentage of GDP rose from an average of 15 percent in 1960 to 26 percent in 1980.* This compares with an average of about 35 percent for the industrial market economies. One reason for the lower budget percentage in LDCs is the much smaller importance of transfer payments. In the industrial market economies, transfer payments constitute about 55 percent of total budget outlays. The corresponding percentage in the middle-income economies is about 15 percent and in low-income countries only a bit over 10 percent. The proportion of the budget going to investment, on the other hand, is substantially higher in these economies than in industrialized countries, averaging 20 percent in middle-income countries and 25 percent in low-income countries, compared with less than 10 percent in the industrial market economies. The LDCs are still building up their capital stock, rather than using their fiscal systems for large-scale redistribution of income.

Little need be said about private consumption. Arithmetically, a rise in the investment and government ratios must mean a decline in the consumption ratio. This decline has been fastest in the high-growth countries. In the 1950s, the median private consumption/GDP ratio in tier 1 and tier 2 countries was about 75 percent. By 1980 this had fallen to 65 percent, not far from typical ratios in the industrialized countries. A corollary is that private consumption per capita has risen a good deal less rapidly than GDP per capita in these countries.

ADDITIONAL DIMENSIONS OF GROWTH: POPULATION, AGRICULTURE, EXPORTS

## Demographic Behavior

I have noted at several points that the deathrate tends to change exogenously, in response mainly to advances in medical science. There was a gradual decline in most countries in the late nineteenth and early twentieth centuries, a marked drop after 1920, and another marked drop after 1945. Table 6 indicates that this process was still going on in the years 1960–80. Over this period the crude deathrate dropped five to ten points in most countries. For tier 1 and tier 2 countries, the

*World Development Report, 1983* (Washington: IBRD, 1983), pp. 47–48.

TABLE 6  Demographic Behavior (births or deaths per thousand)

| Country | Crude Birth Rate | | | Crude Death Rate | | | Rate of Natural Increase | | |
|---|---|---|---|---|---|---|---|---|---|
| | 1960 | 1980 | Change | 1960 | 1980 | Change | 1960 | 1980 | Change |
| South Korea | 43 | 24 | −19 | 13 | 7 | − 6 | 30 | 17 | −13 |
| Taiwan | 40 | 21 | −19 | 7 | 5 | − 2 | 33 | 16 | −17 |
| Iraq | 49 | 45 | − 4 | 20 | 12 | − 8 | 29 | 33 | + 4 |
| Brazil | 43 | 30 | −13 | 13 | 9 | − 4 | 30 | 21 | − 9 |
| Thailand | 44 | 30 | −14 | 15 | 8 | − 7 | 29 | 22 | − 7 |
| Malaysia | 45 | 31 | −14 | 16 | 7 | − 9 | 29 | 24 | − 5 |
| Nigeria | 52 | 50 | − 2 | 25 | 17 | − 8 | 27 | 33 | + 6 |
| Indonesia | 46 | 35 | −11 | 16 | 10 | − 6 | 27 | 22 | − 5 |
| Turkey | 43 | 32 | −11 | 16 | 10 | − 6 | 27 | 22 | − 5 |
| Egypt | 44 | 37 | − 7 | 19 | 12 | − 7 | 25 | 25 | 0 |
| Iran | 46 | 41 | − 5 | 17 | 11 | − 6 | 29 | 30 | + 1 |
| Algeria | 50 | 46 | − 4 | 23 | 13 | −10 | 27 | 33 | + 6 |
| Colombia | 46 | 30 | −16 | 14 | 8 | − 6 | 32 | 22 | −10 |
| Pakistan | 51 | 44 | − 7 | 24 | 16 | −12 | 27 | 28 | + 1 |
| Philippines | 46 | 34 | −12 | 15 | 7 | − 8 | 31 | 27 | − 4 |
| Kenya | 52 | 51 | − 1 | 24 | 13 | −11 | 28 | 38 | +10 |
| Mexico | 45 | 37 | − 8 | 12 | 7 | − 5 | 33 | 30 | − 3 |
| Venezuela | 46 | 35 | −11 | 11 | 6 | − 5 | 35 | 29 | − 6 |
| Ivory Coast | 50 | 47 | − 3 | 26 | 18 | − 8 | 24 | 29 | + 5 |
| Morocco | 52 | 44 | − 8 | 23 | 13 | −10 | 29 | 31 | + 2 |
| Sri Lanka | 36 | 28 | − 8 | 9 | 7 | − 2 | 27 | 21 | − 6 |
| Argentina | 24 | 21 | − 3 | 9 | 8 | − 1 | 15 | 13 | − 2 |
| Tanzania | 47 | 46 | − 1 | 22 | 15 | − 7 | 25 | 31 | + 6 |
| Chile | 37 | 22 | −15 | 12 | 7 | − 5 | 25 | 15 | −10 |
| India | 44 | 36 | − 8 | 22 | 14 | − 8 | 22 | 22 | 0 |
| Ethiopia | 51 | 49 | − 2 | 28 | 24 | − 4 | 23 | 25 | + 2 |
| Burma | 43 | 37 | − 6 | 21 | 14 | − 7 | 22 | 23 | + 1 |
| Peru | 47 | 36 | −11 | 20 | 11 | − 9 | 27 | 25 | − 2 |
| Zimbabwe | 55 | 54 | − 1 | 17 | 13 | − 4 | 38 | 41 | + 3 |
| Zambia | 51 | 49 | − 2 | 24 | 17 | − 7 | 27 | 32 | + 5 |
| Zaire | 48 | 46 | − 2 | 24 | 18 | − 6 | 24 | 28 | + 4 |
| Nepal | 44 | 42 | − 2 | 27 | 20 | − 7 | 17 | 22 | + 5 |
| Mozambique | 46 | 45 | − 1 | 26 | 18 | − 8 | 20 | 27 | + 7 |
| Sudan | 47 | 47 | 0 | 25 | 19 | − 6 | 22 | 28 | + 6 |
| Uganda | 45 | 45 | 0 | 20 | 14 | − 6 | 25 | 31 | + 6 |
| Ghana | 49 | 48 | − 1 | 24 | 17 | − 7 | 25 | 31 | + 6 |
| Afghanistan | 50 | 47 | − 3 | 31 | 26 | − 5 | 19 | 21 | + 2 |
| Medians | | | | | | | | | |
| Tier 1 | 44 | 31.5 | −12.5 | 16 | 9 | − 7 | 29 | 22 | − 7 |
| Tier 2 | 46 | 41 | − 5 | 17 | 11 | − 6 | 29 | 30 | + 1 |
| Tier 3 | 44 | 36 | − 8 | 22 | 13 | − 9 | 22 | 23 | + 1 |
| Tier 4 | 48 | 47 | − 1 | 24 | 18 | − 6 | 24 | 29 | + 5 |

SOURCE: IBRD, *World Development Report,* 1982.

process is substantially completed, their median deathrates now being close to developed-country levels.

It is interesting to note that, although the absolute level of deathrates remains somewhat higher in tier 3 and especially in tier 4 countries, the *decrease* in deathrates from 1960 to 1980 was almost identical for all four tiers. Even the low-growth countries have been able to match the rates of progress in the high-growth countries, partly by drawing on low-cost technical assistance provided by the World Health Organization and other international bodies.

Thus the strong upward pressure on population growth rates, which has been provided by declining mortality since 1900, is now nearing its end. From now on the outcome will hinge mainly on birthrate behavior. Table 6 shows that in 1960 most countries still had birthrates in the 40–50 per thousand range, representing essentially uncontrolled fertility. The only exceptions were relatively high-income Argentina and Chile plus Sri Lanka. Since 1960, the trend has clearly been downward. Only two countries fail to show a drop in the crude birthrate between 1960 and 1980, Uganda and Sudan showing no change. A dozen countries show declines of more than ten points, reaching 19 points in South Korea and Taiwan, a remarkable change for such a short period. The rate of decline in birthrates seems clearly related to the rate of economic growth. Between 1960 and 1980 the median for tier 1 countries dropped 12.5 points, while the median for tier 4 countries fell only one point.

The decline of birthrates in the industrialized countries accompanying their increasing affluence is a familiar story. This process seems now to be setting in throughout most of the third world. The reasons for declining birthrates no doubt differ somewhat from country to country, and many case studies are currently under way. A number of countries have adopted vigorous family-planning pro-grams—China is the most dramatic example—and these have clearly had some effect. But more important in most cases are the factors that were operative earlier in the OECD countries: rising incomes and consumption aspirations, increases in education, improvement in the status of women, urbanization changing the cost-benefit balance from additional children, and so on. At any event, the downtrend in most countries seems well established and likely to continue. The black side of the picture is that the countries with poorest growth performance also show least progress in fertility control. The median birthrate in tier 4 countries in 1980 was still 47 per thousand, with the result that children are appearing in largest numbers in the countries least able to support them.

Changes in the rate of natural increase, shown in the final columns of table 6, reflect the outcome of the race between declining fertility and declining mortality. For tier 1 countries, fertility decline pulled ahead in the race between 1960 and 1980, and the median rate of natural increase dropped from 29 to 22 per thousand. The rate will certainly continue to decline in future. In tier 2 and tier 3 countries, the race was a tie and the median rates of natural increase in 1960 and 1980 were almost identical. But here, too, one can safely predict a decline in the near future.

The most pessimistic prognosis is for tier 4 countries. Here mortality decline won the race by a decisive margin, and the rate of natural increase *rose* by five points. With deathrates still relatively high, there is considerable room for further decline. Thus the population growth rate seems more likely to rise than to fall over the next decade or two.

## Agricultural Output and Food Output

We would expect success in raising agricultural output to be an important determinant of overall growth. For a long time after the turning point agriculture remains the largest sector, so its growth rate has heavy weight in the GDP growth rate. But the relationship is more than arithmetical. Except for a limited number of oil-mineral economies, agriculture is the main source of exports; and the export growth rate, as we shall see, is an important determinant of the GDP growth rate. Domestic food supply is also a critical factor. Failure to raise food production as rapidly as food demand tends to produce a relative rise in food prices, which puts upward pressure on money wages, which tends to reduce industrial profits. A lagging agricultural sector also means that farmers cannot provide a vigorously expanding market for domestic manufactures.

In an open economy, of course, the food constraint is relaxed in two ways. First, part of the country's land is usually devoted to export crops—indeed, basic food crops such as rice may also be important exports. The growth rate of domestic food availabilities can thus be raised by diverting land from nonfood export crops to food crops, or by consuming more of the food output at home and exporting less, or both. A notable example is Burma, which at one time had a large export surplus of rice; this surplus has been shrinking since 1945 as more and more of the rice output is eaten at home. Second, there is the possibility of importing food, which some countries in our sample have used on a substantial scale.

I shall concentrate here on the data on food production in table 7. But note that for well over half the countries in our sample the average growth rate of food output is *above* that of total agricultural output. This suggests that diversion of land from nonfood to food crops has been occurring on a substantial scale. The extent to which food output is being eaten at home rather than exported does not show up in the table, but there is evidence that this has also been happening in quite a few countries.

Examination of table 7 reveals a clear relation between agricultural performance and overall economic performance. The median growth rate of both agricultural output and food output declines steadily as we go from tier 1 to tier 4. There is an especially sharp break between tiers 1 and 2, with median growth rates above 3 percent, and tiers 3 and 4, with median growth rates below 2 percent. The tier 1 and tier 2 countries have also improved their performance over time. Their medians for the 1970s are perceptibly above those for the 1950s. The main reason for the increase is probably the introduction of new agricultural technology—improved seed varieties, more fertilizer, better water control—in many countries from the mid-1960s onward, which has substantially raised yields per acre. But

TABLE 7  Growth Rates of Agricultural Production and Food Production (percent per year)

| Country | Agricultural Production | | | | Food Production | | | |
|---|---|---|---|---|---|---|---|---|
| | 1952–54/ 1959–61 | 1959–61/ 1969–71 | 1969–71/ 1979–81 | 1952–54/ 1979–81 | 1952–54/ 1959–61 | 1959–61/ 1969–71 | 1969–71/ 1979–81 | 1952–54/ 1979–81 |
| South Korea | 5.4 | 3.2 | 4.2 | 4.4 | 4.2 | 4.0 | 4.3 | 4.0 |
| Taiwan | | | | | | | | |
| Iraq | 0.3 | 4.5 | 2.2 | 2.4 | 0.1 | 4.4 | 2.3 | 2.4 |
| Brazil | 4.7 | 2.6 | 4.3 | 3.7 | 4.0 | 4.3 | 4.4 | 4.3 |
| Thailand | 4.5 | 5.1 | 5.1 | 4.8 | 3.2 | 5.3 | 5.4 | 4.6 |
| Malaysia | 3.0[1] | 5.6 | 4.8 | 4.4 | 4.1[1] | 5.3 | 6.1 | 5.1 |
| Nigeria | | | 2.1 | | | | 2.3 | |
| Indonesia | 1.6 | 2.2 | 3.4 | 2.4 | 1.9 | 2.3 | 3.6 | 2.5 |
| Turkey | 3.2 | 3.1 | 3.6 | 3.2 | 3.2 | 3.0 | 3.7 | 3.2 |
| Egypt | 2.8 | 3.4 | 1.2 | 2.4 | 3.1 | 3.8 | 1.5 | 2.7 |
| Iran | 3.9 | 2.8 | 3.5 | 3.2 | 3.1 | 2.6 | 4.0 | 3.1 |
| Algeria | -1.2 | -0.2 | 1.3 | 0.1 | -1.4 | -0.2 | 1.3 | -0.1 |
| Colombia | 2.5 | 3.0 | 4.1 | 3.1 | 1.9 | 3.5 | 4.3 | 3.2 |
| Pakistan | 2.2 | 3.8 | 3.1 | 3.0 | 2.3 | 3.6 | 3.3 | 3.0 |
| Philippines | 3.1 | 3.4 | 4.7 | 3.6 | 3.1 | 3.2 | 4.5 | 3.5 |
| Kenya | | | 3.2 | | | | 2.3 | |
| Mexico | 5.0 | 4.5 | 3.5 | 4.1 | 5.1 | 5.2 | 3.7 | 4.5 |
| Venezuela | 4.5 | 5.3 | 3.8 | 4.4 | 4.8 | 5.7 | 4.0 | 4.7 |
| Ivory Coast | | | 4.6 | | | | 5.1 | |
| Morocco | -0.9 | 4.0 | 1.0 | 1.7 | 0.0 | 3.9 | 1.0 | 1.7 |
| Sri Lanka | 2.4 | 3.0 | 3.5 | 3.0 | 2.5 | 3.9 | 5.7 | 4.0 |
| Argentina | 0.6 | 1.6 | 2.7 | 1.6 | 0.6 | 2.1 | 2.9 | 1.9 |

| | C1 | C2 | C3 | C4 | C5 | C6 | C7 | C8 |
|---|---|---|---|---|---|---|---|---|
| Tanzania | 2.1 | -2.0 | 1.6 | 1.5 | 2.1 | 1.8 | 2.0 | 1.7 |
| Chile | | | 1.3 | | | | 1.4 | |
| | | | | | | | | |
| India | 2.6 | 2.2 | 2.4 | 2.4 | 2.7 | 2.1 | 2.4 | 2.3 |
| Ethiopia | 2.4 | 2.5 | 0.6 | 1.7 | 1.9 | 2.0 | 0.5 | 1.4 |
| Burma | 2.3 | 2.5 | 2.8 | 2.4 | 2.5 | 2.3 | 2.7 | 2.5 |
| Peru | 2.6 | 2.2 | 0.8 | 1.7 | 2.3 | 3.2 | 0.7 | 1.9 |
| | | | | | | | | |
| Zimbabwe | | | 3.2 | | | | 2.7 | |
| Zambia | | | 2.2 | | | | 2.3 | |
| Zaire | | | 1.2 | | | | 1.3 | |
| Nepal | | | 0.7 | | | | 0.8 | |
| Mozambique | | | -1.1 | | | | -0.7 | |
| Sudan | 4.5 | 4.6 | 1.4 | 3.4 | 4.1 | 4.7 | 3.0 | 3.8 |
| Uganda | | | -0.4 | | | | 1.5 | |
| Ghana | | | -0.7 | | | | -0.3 | |
| Afghanistan | 2.7 | 0.5 | 2.0 | 1.6 | 2.6 | 0.2 | 2.2 | 1.5 |
| | | | | | | | | |
| Medians | | | | | | | | |
| Tier 1 | 3.1 | 3.3 | 3.9 | 3.45 | 3.2 | 4.15 | 4.0 | 3.6 |
| Tier 2 | 3.1 | 3.4 | 3.65 | 3.2 | 3.1 | 3.5 | 4.0 | 3.2 |
| Tier 3 | 2.3 | 2.35 | 2.0 | 1.7 | 2.2 | 2.2 | 1.9 | 1.9 |
| Tier 4 | * | * | 1.2 | * | * | * | 1.5 | * |

*too few observations

1West Malaysia only

SOURCES: FAO, *Production Yearbook*, 1955–82.

more-favorable government policies toward agriculture have also contributed. At any event, quite a few of these countries are approaching, or have already reached, a favorable conjuncture of decelerating population growth and accelerating food output. Especially hopeful in this respect are South Korea, Taiwan, Brazil, Thailand, and Malaysia.

Performance has varied widely, both among countries in each decade and from decade to decade in a particular country. A dozen or so countries show steady improvement decade by decade. This group includes Brazil, Colombia, Malaysia, Thailand, Indonesia, Sri Lanka, and Philippines. Another group shows rather steady performance, with no perceptible uptrend. This includes South Korea, Taiwan, India, Turkey, Mexico, and Venezuela. A third group shows deteriorating agricultural performance over the years. These are mainly tier 4 countries, but Chile and Peru are also included.

The low rate of agricultural growth in tier 3 and tier 4 countries is worth underlining for the following reason: the low GDP growth rate of the poorest countries is often attributed to the large weight of their agricultural sector, which tends to grow more slowly than the industrial sector. But the lower growth rate of agriculture itself provides an *additional* reason for their poor performance.

One feature of table 7 may appear puzzling. Many countries were not raising food output fast enough to meet rising consumer demand. How then was demand satisfied? For countries in a strong export position, the main answer was rising imports of food. This is true of all the oil economies in the table and also of prominent mineral exporters, such as Chile and Zambia (copper) and Morocco (phosphates). Here the ready availability of foreign exchange to finance food imports led governments to relax their agricultural effort, a policy that may prove hazardous over the longer run. Another group of countries were able to maintain consumption levels by moderate and intermittent food imports, as in India, or by reducing food exports, as in Burma. Finally, in a regrettable number of countries, the answer was a shrinkage in per capita food consumption. Looking back at table 3 we note that, of the fifteen lowest-ranking countries, ten show a decline in food availability. Seven of these countries are in Africa, where consumption levels generally have been declining despite substantial gifts of food from the developed countries.

## Export Performance

A recurrent theme in this book has been the role of foreign demand in stimulating domestic growth, a role that has continued in the post-1945 period. Table 8 shows two indicators of export growth: the growth rate of merchandise exports decade by decade and the ratio of exports to GDP at the beginning and end of the period under study. The two measures are related, since a growth rate of exports exceeding that of GDP will necessarily raise the export/GDP ratio.

The marked relation between export growth and overall growth is apparent

TABLE 8   Export Performance, 1950–1980

| Country | Growth of Merchandise Exports (percent per year) | | | | Exports/GDP (percent) | | Change (percent of GDP) |
|---|---|---|---|---|---|---|---|
| | 1950–60 | 1960–70 | 1970–80 | 1950–80 | 1950–52 | 1978–80 | |
| South Korea | 1.4 | 39.6 | 37.2 | 29.7 | 1.2 | 28.1 | +26.9 |
| Taiwan | 9.3 | 21.7 | 15.7[12] | | 9.2 | 53.6 | +44.4 |
| Iraq | 14.0 | 5.5 | 40.2 | 14.9 | 24.9 | 58.0[9] | +33.1 |
| Brazil | −2.0 | 7.2 | 21.7 | 8.9 | 9.0 | 9.1 | + 0.1 |
| Thailand | 1.5 | 5.1 | 24.6 | 10.1 | 18.2 | 18.8 | + 0.6 |
| Malaysia | 0.6 | 4.3 | 24.5 | 8.2 | 52.0[3] | 51.7 | − 0.3 |
| Nigeria | 4.1 | 8.1 | 33.1 | 15.3 | 26.5 | 21.1 | − 5.4 |
| Indonesia | −1.1 | 1.7 | 35.3 | 9.8 | 18.4[8] | 31.7 | +13.7 |
| Turkey | 0.0 | 6.0 | 16.2 | 7.7 | 7.6 | 3.9 | − 3.7 |
| Egypt | 0.1 | 4.5 | 12.9 | 5.6 | 19.2 | 10.0 | − 9.2 |
| Iran | 36.4 | 12.6 | 22.9 | 21.2 | 6.0 | 26.8 | +20.8 |
| Algeria | 3.0 | 3.8 | 30.6 | 11.4 | 24.7 | 31.0[10] | + 6.3 |
| Colombia | 0.4 | 4.0 | 19.8 | 6.2 | 12.0 | 13.1 | + 1.1 |
| Pakistan | −4.2 | 10.3 | 13.2 | 6.9 | 8.9 | 9.9 | + 1.0 |
| Philippines | 4.5 | 7.5 | 17.7 | 9.1 | 9.6 | 14.0 | + 4.4 |
| Kenya | 8.0 | 6.8 | 16.9 | 11.0 | 18.5 | 18.6 | + 0.1 |
| Mexico | 3.4 | 5.9 | 25.7 | 8.6 | 9.8 | 6.1 | − 3.7 |
| Venezuela | 8.1 | 1.2 | 19.9 | 7.6 | 34.1 | 26.0 | − 8.1 |
| Ivory Coast | 4.5 | 11.7 | 22.2 | 11.9 | 28.3[5] | 30.1[11] | + 1.8 |
| Morocco | 5.0 | 3.7 | 15.9 | 7.2 | 19.6 | 15.7 | − 3.9 |
| Sri Lanka | 0.9 | −1.4 | 13.0 | 2.5 | 33.9 | 27.7 | − 6.2 |
| Argentina | 2.3 | 5.0 | 20.4 | 7.9 | 5.8 | 10.8 | − 5.0 |
| Tanzania | 3.5 | 5.0 | 7.6 | 5.7 | 26.0[2] | 10.9 | −15.1 |
| Chile | 3.7 | 10.2 | 16.0 | 7.9 | 15.3 | 17.8 | + 2.5 |
| India | 0.0 | 3.7 | 15.9 | 6.0 | 6.7[7] | 4.9 | − 1.8 |
| Ethiopia | 6.6 | 5.1 | 13.6 | 7.6 | 7.6[6] | 9.9 | + 2.3 |
| Burma | 1.0 | −8.8 | 14.1 | −0.2 | 20.6 | 6.2 | −14.4 |
| Peru | 6.2 | 8.4 | 13.9 | 9.0 | 18.0 | 25.6 | + 7.6 |
| Zimbabwe | 5.3 | 5.6 | 12.9 | 9.0 | n.a. | 25.6 | n.a. |
| Zambia | 6.6 | 13.4 | 4.7 | 7.3 | 74.6 | 36.4 | −38.2 |
| Zaire | 4.5 | 6.1 | 7.9 | 4.9 | 38.8 | 20.8 | −18.0 |
| Nepal | | | | | | 6.0[11] | n.a. |
| Mozambique | 6.2 | 7.0 | −4.0 | 5.2 | | | n.a. |
| Sudan | 2.6 | 3.4 | 7.4 | 5.5 | 17.5[4] | 7.0 | −10.5 |
| Uganda | 3.1 | 7.1 | 4.2 | 5.2 | 27.9[1] | 4.2 | −23.7 |
| Ghana | 3.1 | 2.2 | 10.9 | 5.4 | 32.2 | 10.4[10] | −21.8 |
| Afghanistan | 2.6 | 4.3 | 20.6 | 8.2 | 4.1 | 11.7[10] | + 7.6 |

(*continued*)

[1]1950   [2]1954   [3]1955   [4]1956–58   [5]1960–62   [6]1961   [7]1966–68   [8]1967   [9]1975
[10]1977   [11]1978   [12]1970–77

SOURCES: Columns 1–4: UNCTAD, *Handbook of International Trade and Development Statistics,* various issues. Columns 5–6: *UN Yearbook of International Trade Statistics,* 1980; IMF, *International Financial Statistics,* various issues; IBRD, *World Tables,* 1980; Taiwan [Republic of China], *National Income of the Republic of China, 1982.*

TABLE 8    *(continued)*

| Country | Growth of Merchandise Exports (percent per year) | | | | Exports/GDP (percent) | | Change (percent of GDP) |
|---------|---------|---------|---------|---------|---------|---------|---------|
|         | *1950–60* | *1960–70* | *1970–80* | *1950–80* | *1950–52* | *1978–80* | |
| Medians |         |         |         |         |         |         |         |
| Tier 1  | 1.0     | 6.0     | 24.5    | 10.0    | 18.3    | 24.6    |         |
| Tier 2  | 4.5     | 6.8     | 19.9    | 9.1     | 12.0    | 18.6    |         |
| Tier 3  | 3.5     | 5.0     | 14.1    | 7.2     | 18.0    | 10.9    |         |
| Tier 4  | 3.8     | 5.8     | 7.9     | 5.2     | 30.0    | 11.1    |         |

from table 8. Over the period 1950–80, the median growth rate of exports was 10.0 percent per year in tier 1 countries and 9.1 percent in tier 2 countries, compared with only 5.2 percent in tier 4 countries. Even if we omit the oil economies as well as the spectacular cases of South Korea and Taiwan, most tier 1 and tier 2 countries managed to increase exports at rates of 7–11 percent per year. The median export/GDP ratio for both groups rose substantially, while for the two lower tiers it deteriorated.

The reasons for high export growth rates differ from country to country, but two factors deserve special emphasis. The first is a tendency during the 1960s and 1970s for one country after another to turn away from highly restrictive trade policies toward outward-looking policies more favorable to exports. These reform "packages" typically included such elements as: adoption of a unified and realistic exchange rate and in some cases a floating or "crawling peg" system; reduction of tariff rates and import quotas; liberalization or abandonment of foreign-exchange allocation systems; and new export incentives such as tax rebates, cheap credit, and free import of raw materials and capital goods. The result was to raise the profitability of exports relative to import-substituting activities, and exports typically responded strongly. Countries that moved in this direction include Taiwan, South Korea, Brazil, Colombia, Pakistan, Turkey, Egypt, and Sri Lanka. A number of other countries, such as Malaysia and Thailand, had always been export-oriented and simply continued their liberal trade policies.

The second important fact is that countries that adopted policies favorable to exports were generally successful not only in raising exports of primary products, but also in penetrating the world market for manufactures. The spectacular examples are South Korea and Taiwan, where manufactures now form 90 percent of total exports. But quite a few other countries have succeeded in raising exports of manufactures from a few percent to 20 percent or more of total exports as of 1980. Examples include Mexico (25.5 percent), Brazil (32.6 percent), Pakistan (48.2 percent), Egypt (19.7 percent), Thailand (22.6 percent), Turkey (26.2 percent), Philippines (21.6 percent), Colombia (19.6 percent), and Sri Lanka (18.6 percent). Manufactured exports are continuing to rise more rapidly than traditional exports, and these percentages will be considerably higher by 1990.

Although we have data also on merchandise imports, little would be gained by presenting them here. In general, the import/GDP ratio tracks the export/GDP ratio, rising where exports are buoyant, falling where exports are doing poorly. Most countries have a deficit on merchandise trade in most years; and except for the oil economies these deficits, as a percentage of GDP, were typically larger in 1978–80 than they had been in 1950–52. Deficits are closed in a variety of ways. Some countries now benefit greatly from remittances from their nationals employed abroad (Turkey, Egypt, Sudan, Pakistan, Sri Lanka, Mexico). Kenya, Mexico, and a few others have substantial revenues from tourism. But the trade gap is closed mainly by transfers of short-term and longer-term capital. Some idea of the size of these transfers can be obtained from the final two columns of table 5. These "resource balance" columns show the export surplus ($+$) or deficit ($-$) as a percentage of the country's GDP.

### WHY DO GROWTH RATES DIFFER?

Although our tables suggest factors that may have had an important effect on country growth rates, one would like to have some measure of their relative importance. The standard procedure is to regress the growth rate against possible explanatory variables. I selected twelve variables that might plausibly be related to economic growth and ran a large number of regressions to test their significance. As one might expect, some of these variables turned out not to be statistically significant. The ordinary least-squares regression, which performed best for the countries examined, was as follows:

$$\text{GNP growth rate} = -0.5 + 0.8 \text{ agricultural production growth rate}$$
$$(2.4)$$
$$+ 0.09 \text{ export growth rate}$$
$$(2.8)$$
$$- 0.005 \text{ population density in 1960}$$
$$(-0.8)$$
$$+ 0.01 \text{ GDI/GDP growth rate.}$$
$$(1.7)$$

All growth rates are annual average growth rates from 1960 to 1980. The GNP figures used are the World Bank estimates shown in table 2. It turned out not to matter much whether the growth rate of GNP or of GNP per capita was used as the dependent variable. The coefficients and $t$-statistics were very similar in the two cases. GDI/GDP is the share of gross domestic investment in gross domestic product. $R^2$ is equal to 0.70, and it is significant at 1.2 percent.

In general, the variables that emerged as significant were those which stand out in the tables presented earlier. Together, success in promoting (merchandise) exports, encouraging agriculture, and increasing the share of investment in national income accounts for about 70 percent of growth in GNP over the twenty-year period.

Some degree of multicollinearity between the variables has lowered their individual significance. This mattered particularly, as might be expected, for the investment and agriculture variables; the importance of both rose significantly as one or.the other was dropped. Nonetheless, except for population density, all explanatory variables were, even in this equation, significant at the 10 percent level. Tested separately, they were all significant at the 1 percent level.

So, as noted earlier, international competitiveness matters for growth, as do both the level (result not shown) and growth rate of investment, though the direction of causality between these latter and GNP growth is not clear. The existence of a healthy agricultural sector is probably both a reflection of and a catalyst to growth.

The variable used for population density was hectares of arable land per head of population in 1960. I surmised that a country with less arable land per capita might on this account have a lower growth rate. This hypothesis is weakly supported here. It appears that, when a zero restriction is imposed on the density variable, the negative effect of increasing population density is found in company with, and offsets to some extent, the positive effects of high investment and exports.

Several apparently plausible hypotheses were not confirmed by the analysis. Population growth is often assumed to operate as a drag on progress, in the sense that a higher population growth rate is negatively related to growth of output per capita. I ran a variety of regressions—for GNP, for GNP per capita, for the entire period, for several decades—using the population growth rate as independent variable. None of these yielded significant results. This is in line with Kuznets's (1966) earlier findings for a sample of "developed" countries over the period 1860–1960, in which he found no significant relation between growth rates of population and per capita income.

Again, one might think that it is easier for a small country to develop than for a large country. This theory was tested using 1960 population as a crude indicator of size. The coefficient was insignificant. Or one might expect a low-income country to grow faster than a high-income country, on the basis of a "catching-up" hypothesis. But income per capita in 1960 did not prove to be significantly related to the 1960–80 growth rate.

### Missing Variables: The Political Element

Even though we know that growth of agricultural output, growth and diversification of exports, and a high investment rate seem to be important, the sources of sustained growth remain mysterious. It is clear from table 5 that countries with apparently similar investment rates can have very different growth rates. Compare

Brazil and Tanzania, or Thailand and India. Some countries extract more output from capital than do others. An effort to explain why quickly leads us beyond the boundaries of economic analysis.

Some of the most important variables excluded from economic models can be labeled as political. Government matters. When we ask in precisely what ways it matters, the answer seems to include at least the following: strength of nationhood; degree of continuity in political leadership; degree of interest in economic growth by the governing group; administrative competence of government; and general stance of economic policy. Without professing to be at all complete, I shall turn now to exploring these variables.

1. *Nationhood.* The term *nation* carries connotations derived from Western experience, which are often inappropriate in the third-world setting. In Europe and North America, a nation was a well-defined geographic area whose residents usually shared a common language and a sense of cultural identity. This sense of nationhood had been consolidated gradually over the centuries, usually before the outset of intensive growth.

Third-world countries range all the way from those which are nations in the full sense to those which are scarcely nations at all. The Latin American countries have substantial linguistic and cultural unity, though in some countries the admixture of European and Indian groups has produced social and political stratification. They also have a tradition of self-government over a century and a half. Some Asian countries—Japan, China, Korea, Thailand—also have a strong sense of national identity. But India, more nearly a continent than a country, has great ethnic and religious diversity; and so do Indonesia, Malaysia, the Philippines, and some other Asian countries. Diversity is even more evident in sub-Saharan Africa. Here the precolonial political boundaries were tribal, and the new boundaries drawn by the colonial powers were quite artificial. Tribal allegiances persisted during the colonial period, which in any event was rather short, and have been affirmed strongly in the era of independence. African governments today often represent a large and dominant tribe, and other tribes remain outside the power structure.

Thus for the ordinary person in Africa, in many parts of Asia, and even in certain Indian regions of Latin America, the notion that the government is "his" government, or that he should make sacrifices for the future of "his" country, probably has little acceptance. This alienation is reinforced by the fact that most third-world countries are governed by a military group, a civilian oligarchy, or even a personal monarch. A continuous tradition of selecting government leaders through open and broadly based elections is unusual. The inability of many governments to rely on a developed sense of citizenship, and their consequent inability to mobilize initiative or impose economic sacrifices for the sake of national goals, is characteristic of what Myrdal has labeled "the soft state."

2. *Continuity of Political Leadership.* The need for continuity is almost self-

evident. Frequent and abrupt transfers of power make it difficult to develop a coherent economic strategy. They may also involve loss of life, destruction of property, and disruption of production.

Continuity can be and is achieved in a variety of ways: through peaceable transfer of power as a result of elections, as in India, Sri Lanka, Malaysia, and (recently) Colombia and Venezuela; through continuous rule by a single dominant party, as in Mexico, Ivory Coast, Tanzania, Kenya, Algeria, and Taiwan, plus China and other communist-led countries; through personal dictatorship, usually by a military leader, as in South Korea, Indonesia, Pakistan, Iraq, Zaire, and (recently) Argentina, Brazil, and Chile; or through a personal monarchy, as in Nepal, pre-1978 Iran, and Morocco.

Dislike of military government is (rightly) built into American ways of thought. But I have not seen clear evidence that military rule *per se* is either favorable or adverse to economic growth. It should be noted that in some third-world countries the army is virtually the only effective administrative organization; that it provides one of the few channels by which an able young man from a poor family can rise to a position of leadership; and that, since it uses modern technology embodied in modern weapons, it serves to develop both technical skills and attitudes favorable to modernization throughout the economy.* One can easily construct a box score of countries which have progressed substantially under military rule, as in Brazil, Pakistan, Indonesia, and South Korea, as against countries in which military rule has debauched the economy, as in Argentina, Uganda, Ghana, and Zaire. But such anecdotal evidence is scarcely conclusive.

A number of countries, particularly in Africa, have had a turbulent political history, including anticolonial wars, civil wars, coups and countercoups. Examples are Ghana, Nigeria, Uganda, and Mozambique, where political instability in itself is sufficient to explain mediocre or poor economic performance. But neither does stability necessarily provide any *guarantee* of growth. The governments of Burma under the generals, Nepal under the king, Ethiopia in the Haile Selassie era, and Zaire under Mobutu have been quite stable, but growth has been minimal. Continuity of leadership seems to be a necessary but not a sufficient condition for good performance.

3. *Orientation of Leadership.* The interests and orientation of the governing group can also be decisive for economic growth. Historically, most governments have concentrated on staying in power, putting down dissenters, and perhaps making war on neighboring nations. Attaching high priority to economic progress might be regarded as unusual, even eccentric. Yet it does happen. It makes a difference whether government is dominated by a landowning class interested mainly in drawing customary rents from the land or whether merchants and

---

*See Lucian W. Pye, "Armies in the Process of Political Modernization," in *The Role of the Military in Underdeveloped Countries,* ed. John J. Johnson (Princeton: Princeton University Press, 1962).

nascent industrialists also have substantial influence. The growing power of the mercantile-industrial bourgeoisie was very important in northwestern Europe, North America, and Japan in the nineteenth century; and it is important today in most Latin American and some Asian countries.

Nationalist motivation—economic growth as a basis for national independence and military power—has been important on occasion, notably in Japan and China. In South Korea and Taiwan, fear of "the enemy" has reinforced leadership pleas for economic effort. In communist-led countries, of course, economic growth is a secular religion, and effort in this direction can be taken for granted.

4. *Administrative Competence.* A key requirement for success is a competent administrative staff, not only at top government levels but at lower levels as well, so that policies and projects developed at the top are carried out effectively. All the requisites for economic progress—effective collection of taxes, execution of public works and other infrastructure projects, dissemination of modern technology and inputs to farmers, expansion of education and health facilities—require competence and continuity in staffing. The capacity of third-world governments in this respect ranges all the way from near-European levels to virtually zero. The difficulties of most African countries arise partly from the fact that colonial administrative staffs were dominated by Europeans with little African participation. Thus when the Europeans departed they left almost a vacuum, which will take a long time to fill. In India, on the other hand, economic performance has been aided by the strong professional tradition of the Indian civil service, which over the years came to consist increasingly of Indian rather than British personnel. If one could develop a quantitative indicator of administrative capacity, it would probably show a high correlation with economic performance.

A much-discussed question, which cannot be considered adequately here, is the widespread acceptance of bribes by public officials. This sometimes arises from low civil-service salaries, which over time tend to be eroded by inflation and which must be supplemented in some way to provide even a minimal standard of living. Another source is the tendency of third-world governments to regulate private economic activity in detail. When almost any transaction requires a license, or a permit, or a ration, or an allocation of inputs or foreign exchange, there is a natural tendency to speed the transaction by a payment to the official in charge. The payment may be to get him to do something that is already his duty (tipping the postman to get delivery of your letter), to speed up a legitimate transaction, to get preferential treatment where claimants exceed supplies, or to get an extralegal exception to the rules. Such payments have sometimes been defended as necessary grease on the wheels of a slow-moving bureaucracy. But they also introduce an element of uncertainty. How much must I pay? Will it work? And they can even cause a slowdown of action, as when a bureaucrat declines to do anything until the right payment is forthcoming. Myrdal, after looking at the matter closely in the Asian setting, reached a clearly negative verdict.

A particular weakness in most third-world countries is a shortage of middle management. There may be good economic technocrats at the top of the govern-ment structure but, as one goes down the hierarchy, capacity diminishes rapidly. The result can be what Latin Americans call "projectismo"—the development of ambitious plans at the top that are executed only partially or not at all. Thus along with considering what government *should* do, given an ample supply of angelic administrators, one must always bear in mind what government is *able* to do in the real world.

5. *Policy Stance*. By *policy stance* I mean mainly the extent to which govern-ment encourages and relies on private economic initiative or, on the contrary, the extent to which it tries to substitute government decisions for private decisions. There is evidence that such policy orientation can have substantial effect on the growth rate. Where government concentrates on maintaining an appropriate struc-ture of incentives and relies on private economic agents to respond, the production response is usually strong. On the other hand, an effort to control private economic activity in detail usually has a stultifying effect. This point is so important that I shall devote most of the next chapter to exploring it and so will say nothing more here.

These five variables might be regarded as measurable, in principle, with values ranging from 1 to 0 for a particular country. It was tempting to try to assign numerical grades to each country on each variable and to see whether the consoli-dated scores were closely related to growth rates. But to do this at all accurately would have meant much additional research and consultations with country spe-cialists, which time did not permit.*

On an impressionistic basis, however, the importance of political variables stands out strongly. Omitting the oil economies, the top five performers in table 2 are South Korea, Taiwan, Brazil, Thailand, and Malaysia. It would be fair to characterize all these countries as displaying the following traits: a strong sense of national identity (though with some Chinese-Malay dissension in Malaysia); con-tinuity of political leadership (though with a civilian-military shift in Brazil in 1964 and occasional disturbances in Thailand moderated by the influence of the king); a growth orientation of leadership, partly because of the influence of a business middle class in these countries; good institutions of higher education and competent administrative staffs (though perhaps least strong in Thailand); a favor-able view of private economic activity and generally astute economic policies.

Look on the other hand at the nine countries with lowest growth rates (tier 4 in table 2). In varying degrees these countries are characterized by: weak national identity; serious political instability (except in Nepal, where the stability is that of an old-fashioned oriental kingdom); leadership that is either uninterested in eco-nomic growth or unable to pursue it effectively; poor performance in higher

*For an interesting effort at quantification of political and social variables, using A–D ratings, see Irma Adelman and Cynthia Taft Morris, *Society, Politics, and Economic Development: A Quantitative Approach* (Baltimore: Johns Hopkins University Press, 1967).

education and administrative staffing; and a tendency to overregulation, which discourages private activity (least evident in Nepal, most evident in Ghana, Zambia, and Uganda under Amin).

Overall, then, consideration of political variables brings us closer to an explanation of growth performance than we could get by looking at economic variables alone.

## A Concluding Word

We all know that statistical association does not reveal causation. Examination of table 5, for example, suggests that countries with apparently similar investment rates can have very different growth rates. Compare Brazil and Tanzania, or Thailand and India. Some countries clearly extract more output from capital than do others. But to explain why would lead us beyond the bounds of regression analysis.

The variables analysts have been unable to quantify seem largely political— continuity of governments, growth orientation (or its absence) in the political leadership, administrative competence of government, effectiveness of policies in agriculture, foreign trade, and other key sectors. The importance of these things is almost self-evident from table 2. Of the twenty countries with highest 1960–80 growth rates, most (not all) would get good scores on political stability, administrative staffing, and effectiveness of economic policies. But the opposite is true of the nine countries in tier 4. Almost all these countries have been wracked by civil wars, by coups and countercoups, or by serious misgovernment and major policy errors. The only country in the group that has enjoyed political stability is Nepal, but this is the stability of an oriental kingdom that cheerfully accepts foreign aid from all comers but otherwise shows minimal interest in economic development.

For good or ill, government seems central to economic growth. For this reason I will devote the final chapter to government activity.

# 6

## The Functions of Government

In the long tradition of political economy, economists have always taken account of government actions. But the tone of the discussion has changed over the years. In the eighteenth and early nineteenth centuries, government was the enemy. The problem was to liberate private production and exchange from the stranglehold of government controls. This emancipation of the market was in large measure accomplished, and most economists thought that it contributed to acceleration of growth in the now "developed" countries. Even Marx looked to capitalism to transform heavily agricultural economies into modern industrial states. Socialism would arrive only after capitalism had developed a powerful engine of production.

Even after free-market economies were in place, government was of course always in the background. It was expected to protect life and property and to establish a legal framework for economic activity. It usually went ahead pragmatically to encourage development of railroads and other infrastructure. It provided national defense, plus a growing amount of education and other public services, financing these activities by a tax system. These minimal functions of government continue in today's developing countries, and we shall largely take them for granted.

In the late nineteenth century government began to reemerge as a more prominent economic actor. The spread of socialist ideas, the gradual extension of the suffrage, a growing popular belief that economic performance was somehow the responsibility of government, all contributed to this trend. The expansion of government functions took several forms: use of taxation and public expenditure to redistribute income; some expansion of public ownership of industry; an increase in the number of wages and prices subjected to public control; a retreat from the high point of free trade around 1870 and a partial return to mercantilist policies; acceptance of government responsibility for the general level of output and employment after the debacle of the Great Depression.

This trend toward creeping interventionism of the state in economic affairs was considerably accelerated by the two world wars. War is the great socializer. Nations discovered that the private economy could be subjected to detailed public control. They discovered also that the tax system could yield revenues much in excess of previous expectations and, as military demands abated, these revenues left room for increased government spending in other directions. In most countries (except for the United States, Canada, and Japan) socialist parties began to alternate in office with conservative parties; and although government functions were sometimes cut back a bit by conservative regimes, the expansionist trend continued.

These changes in the older industrial countries set the stage for economic policy in third-world countries after 1945. In most countries it was accepted with little debate that government is the main instrument for promoting economic development. The old enemy, government, had become the friend and promoter of economic progress. The reasons for this drastic shift from the view held (and practiced) in the older industrial countries during their takeoff periods would form an interesting chapter in the history of economic thought; but I cannot write that chapter here. Rather, I shall examine how well the expanded functions of government are being performed and how fully the record warrants the new faith in government's competence and beneficence.

### THE FRAMEWORK OF ECONOMIC INSTITUTIONS

It would be hard to say anything new or interesting about the conventional functions of government—as tax gatherer, infrastructure builder, and supplier of public services—beyond what has been said in earlier chapters. I shall simply take these functions for granted. But I must comment briefly on an important function that is often overlooked: development of an effective framework of economic institutions. I have in mind here a "mixed economy," in which most productive equipment is privately owned and most economic transactions take place in private markets. What economic institutions are needed in such an economy, and how can government midwife their development?

The concept of a competitive, price-guided, market economy is an attractive utopia, one that has been perfected by economists over more than two centuries. Many people fall in love with it and, in so doing, fall into several kinds of error. The results of the market machinery depend partly on initial conditions, notably the distribution of asset ownership, and what constitutes a proper distribution of wealth cannot be decided on economic grounds alone. There is a tendency to understate the imperfection of markets, the importance of public goods and external economies, and other things that may require government action. Finally, there is a tendency to think that the highly developed market institutions that we see in the more-developed countries sprang spontaneously from the brow of Zeus—or of Adam Smith. But in fact they evolved over a long period; and in third-world countries, at the outset of economic growth, they are usually quite underdeveloped. The most basic task of government—assuming that the goal is a (mainly) private economy—is to foster laws, procedures, and organizations that encourage private initiative and enable producers to reap its rewards.

Since agriculture is usually the largest sector, the institutions governing land ownership and use are especially important. Many third-world economies have always had a system of family farming, which permits effective operation of income incentives. This is true in some (not all) Latin American countries, in most of Africa (where land use is allocated to families even when ownership remains tribal), and in most of Southeast Asia. Some other countries in which land ownership was initially quite unequal have undergone land reforms, as in Taiwan, South Korea, Egypt, and Mexico. Though these reforms differ in detail, they typically involve some combination of (1) subdivision of large, often absentee-managed landholdings into smaller, family-sized units; (2) provision for tenants to become farm owners through long-term government financing; and (3) arrangements for giving the remaining tenants greater security of tenure, a larger share of output, better access to credit, and greater economic independence. Such a re-structuring, which enables the cultivator to make price-guided production deci-sions and to reap the rewards of innovation, seems to be a necessary, though not a sufficient, condition for raising productivity in agriculture. In some countries, particularly in Latin America, the distribution of ownership is still quite unequal; and this is a source of lagging output growth as well as political instability.

In the area of industry and trade there is need for a legal and judicial system to protect property, to ensure enforceability of contracts, and to permit modern forms of business organization. There are still countries in which debts are not legally collectable and where in consequence a person can go into business only with family members over whom he has some moral hold. Thus large private enter-prises are almost precluded. Development of the corporate form was vital to growth of large-scale industry in the presently developed countries; and spread of this form can be expected to play a similar role in third-world economies.

A further need is creation of a modern financial structure. A developing country does not need instant Wall Street. But it does need a central bank; a system of commercial banks, lending preferably at flexible, market-determined rates; facilities for long-term investment finance, usually including one or more govern-ment development banks; a system of savings institutions providing security and an attractive real rate of interest; and a public market for government securities, which can gradually be extended to cover high-grade private securities.

Another important institution is the government's own budget-making ma-chinery. In the economies we are considering here, government usually produces 10–15 percent of national output, and it often accounts for one-third to one-half of gross capital formation. We tend to assume that resources flowing through govern-ment channels will be allocated rationally; but this cannot be taken for granted. It is quite possible for the allocation to be whimsical and unstable, following lines of personal influence rather than any economic rationale. The critical factor here is the top political leadership. Bad leadership cannot be remedied by redrawing organization charts. But given reasonable competence and continuity in lead-ership, one can design budget procedures that will aid rational decision-making.

Rationalization of government's role in the economy is the main function of the multiyear "development plans" used by many third-world countries in recent decades. While these plans are professed to be global, containing macroeconomic targets for the entire economy, their control power over the private sector is usually quite limited. The "hard" part of a development plan relates to the public sector and is essentially a multiyear budget, covering capital expenditures and often current expenditures as well, which serves as a guide for preparation of annual budgets. Making development plans directs attention to long-run priorities rather than simply to immediate pressures. It requires each department of government to document its budget requests more fully and to relate this year's budget to the preceding and following years. This can scarcely fail to improve resource allocation.

The institutional requirements for economic development by the capitalist route were outlined long ago by John Stuart Mill (1848) in a passage that is still highly relevant:

> The desideratum for such a [less-developed] country, economically consid- ered, is an increase of industry and of the effective desire of accumulation. The means are, first, a better government; more complete security of proper- ty; moderate taxes, and freedom from arbitrary exaction under the name of taxes; a more permanent and more advantageous tenure of land, securing to the cultivator as far as possible the undivided benefits of the industry, skill, and economy he may exert. Secondly, improvement of the public intel- ligence. . . . Third, the introduction of foreign arts, which raise the returns derivable from additional capital . . . and the importation of foreign capital, which renders the increase of production no longer exclusively dependent on the thrift or providence of the inhabitants themselves . . . and by instilling new ideas and breaking the chains of habit . . . tends to create in them new wants, increased ambition, and greater thought for the future. These consid- erations apply more or less to all the Asiatic populations, and to the less civilized and industrious parts of Europe, as Russia, Turkey, Spain, and Ireland.

Most of what we talk about today—orderly government, land reform, a tax system that does not encroach unduly on incentives, technology transfer, foreign aid, capital accumulation, rising consumer expectations—is encompassed in Mill's meaty paragraph.

In this as in so many other respects, Japan is the model of a successfully developing economy. Between 1868 and 1900 the Japanese government created almost from scratch a new institutional structure that provided a favorable setting for private economic initiative. Major reforms included abolition of the rigid system of five social classes, membership in which was determined by birth and each of which was limited to prescribed economic activities, and substitution of a more fluid class structure open to men of talent from diverse social origins; abolition of barriers to internal movement of goods and people and dissolution of the restrictive craft guilds; displacement of the feudal lords who, in lieu of their former revenues from agriculture, received allotments of government bonds whose value was later eroded by inflation; replacement of farmers' payments in kind to the feudal lords by a land tax payable in cash to government and simultaneous abolition of the Tokugawa prohibition against the purchase and sale of land; creation of a modern banking system under the National Bank Act of 1872, accompanied by retirement of the many varieties of Tokugawa paper money and their replacement by a single currency; and development of an efficient budgetary system, which for the first time permitted forecasting and control of revenues and expenditures.

POLICIES TOWARD AGRICULTURE

I have already noted the importance of a tenure system that encourages owner-occupied farms of moderate size and, to the extent that tenant farming continues, provides security of tenure and reasonable rent payments. Why does government need to do any more than this? There is abundant evidence that small farmers are shrewd managers, quite responsive to price signals and to demonstrated possibilities for raising their incomes. So why not just leave them alone to operate as they will?

The problem is that, although agricultural production can be organized efficiently on a small scale, it requires a variety of supporting services that must be organized on a larger scale, and indeed must often be organized by government. The most important of these are:

1. Large-scale programs for water supply, drainage, and other land improvements. These usually require concerted action over an area embracing many farms, as well as large capital investment.
2. Infrastructure investments serving agricultural areas, such as farm-to-market roads, warehouses, and other marketing facilities.
3. Farm credit, especially important where improved technology requires larger purchases of fertilizer and other modern inputs, which farmers with small or zero cash reserves have difficulty in financing. Government can promote the formation of credit cooperatives, which have been quite successful in some countries. Government can also encourage extension of commercial bank lending to rural areas—for example, by *not* imposing interest-rate ceilings that make lending unprofitable, discourage saving, and misallocate capital; or it can set up a system of government-operated farm credit banks.
4. Special mention should be made of agricultural research and extension, which has loomed as increasingly important since 1945. New agricultural technology is a public good in the sense that, once developed, it becomes available to all comers. No one farmer can hope to appropriate it or keep it secret. Further, the social return is usually much larger than any private return to the developer. It

is thus necessary for government to assume main responsibility for agricultural research and development. I should note also that improved technology cannot simply be borrowed from the developed countries or from international research centers. Technology always needs to be adapted to specific soil, rainfall, and sunshine conditions within countries, regions, and districts. Effective borrowing and adaptation thus depends on a strong local network of research centers and experiment stations. Evenson and others have done cross-sectional analyses of countries and of individual states within India. These studies suggest a strong relation between agricultural research activity and rates of increase in agricultural productivity. Rates of return to research activity are typically very high, suggesting that research is usually underfinanced.

This catalog is helpful in detecting ways in which a government may go wrong. It may easily go wrong through neglect, through failing to do the things we have specified as important in stimulating farm output. This may happen because large oil or mineral exports make it easy for the time being to finance food imports, with the result that raising domestic food output does not seem very important. Thus it is not surprising that notable cases of agricultural neglect include oil-exporting Venezuela, Algeria, Iraq, and Nigeria and mineral-exporting Chile, Peru, and Zambia. Neglect may also reflect ideological bias, a view that industry is the hope of the future and that agriculture is naturally a backward and inferior sector. The fact that government is often dominated by city people responsive mainly to pressure from urban interests may be a contributing factor. There may even be an element of laziness—it is easier to build a steel mill than to raise agricultural productivity.

A second way in which government may go wrong involves control of farm prices and farm marketings. This is not common practice in Latin America, but it is practiced by most African and some Asian countries.

In these countries basic food crops, as well as major export crops, are typically bought by a government marketing board at a fixed price. The marketing board is also usually responsible for distributing fertilizer, seeds, and other inputs to the farmers, and it sometimes even distributes consumer goods. The system is supposed to "protect" the peasant against the rapacious middleman, who is portrayed as a monopsonistic buyer enforcing an unduly low price at the farm gate. A second argument is that the fixed price protects farmers against the large world-price fluctuations for primary products. The quantities procured by the marketing board are either exported or resold to domestic consumers, often at a subsidized price.

While such a system may protect farmers against exploitation by private traders, the extent of which is usually exaggerated, it facilitates an even more serious exploitation by government. It would be possible in principle to stabilize prices without affecting their average level over the years. But in practice there is an irresistible temptation to use the system as a method of *taxation,* by systematically paying farmers less than world-price levels and less than they would receive in a free domestic market. The size of this tax varies among countries, but it is usually substantial. It is not unusual to find farmers receiving only half to three-quarters of the world price for their produce.

Further, arbitrary setting of *relative* prices for various farm products can lead to substantial misallocation of resources. Farmers are quite responsive to shifts in relative prices, reallocating their land among products so as to maximize private profit. But this allocation may be socially inefficient, that is, it may produce an output bundle inferior in total value to that which would have resulted from farmer response to market-determined prices. In addition to misallocation among major crops, one often finds an abnormal increase in output of "minor" farm products exempted from price control and government procurement. The free prices for these products often rise to very profitable levels, leading farmers to devote more land and labor to them. The effect is not unlike that in China or the Soviet Union, where farmers lavish time on their private plots, whose produce can be sold at uncontrolled prices.

The cumbersome marketing-board system often leads to higher marketing costs and other inefficiencies. Inability to move the crop promptly at harvest time can lead to crop spoilage. Failure to supply inputs at the time they are needed in the production cycle can also reduce production. The much-maligned private middleman would probably do a better job in most cases. Research studies—for example, studies of rice marketing in Thailand and elsewhere—suggest that private markets are usually (not always) competitive, that traders do not have strong monopsony power, and that their profit margins are small.

Agricultural policies are often reinforced by other policies that reduce farm incomes relative to urban incomes. Many countries have maintained an over-valued exchange rate, which reduces the return in domestic currency of all exports, including agricultural exports. At the same time, tariffs and other trade restrictions raise the price to farmers of manufactured goods and agricultural inputs. The combined effect is often a downtrend in the rural-urban terms of trade, which can scarcely encourage farm production.

This depressing effect has been felt most severely in Africa. For all the sub-Saharan African countries, the median annual rate of increase in agricultural output from 1970 to 1979 was only 1.8 percent, well below the rate of population growth. In addition to countries in the Sahel, which were affected by drought, several other countries show an actual drop in agricultural output during the decade. The list includes Mozambique, Ghana, Zimbabwe, Angola, and Nigeria. A World Bank study* attributes this poor showing partly to inadequate income incentives to farmers. In Tanzania, for example, official prices paid to producers have not kept pace with world prices or domestic production costs. The terms of trade for cash-crop farmers fell by almost one-third during the 1970s. The story is

*Accelerated Development in Sub-Saharan Africa* (Washington: The World Bank, 1981).

similar in Ghana. Between 1965 and 1979 cocoa output fell by almost 60 percent, and Ghana's share of the world market dropped from one-third to one-sixth. One reason must be that the price paid by the Cocoa Marketing Board rose only sixfold, whereas the price index for consumer goods was rising 22 times. As a result farmers have been neglecting their cocoa trees, trying to shift into other crops, and smuggling cocoa to neighboring countries offering much higher prices.

But we should not paint the picture blacker than it is. Horror stories about agricultural policy can be matched by perhaps an equal number of favorable cases. Ivory Coast has always been proagriculture and proexport. The president, himself owner of a large farm, requires each of his cabinet members to own 12.5 acres of farmland, and each member of parliament must own 7.5 acres. Mexico, in addition to its major land reform, invested heavily in rural infrastructure from 1930 onward and has also been unusually active in agricultural research and development. In Taiwan, the active agricultural policy initiated by the Japanese has continued into the independence period. In addition to the land reform of the early 1950s, government has pursued a comprehensive development policy involving improvement of rural health and education, development of agricultural research and extension, expansion of irrigation facilities, development of farmers' self-help organizations and government lending institutions, and provision of growing amounts of modern inputs. Malaysia, in addition to a massive program of rubber-tree replanting, has moved energetically to raise domestic food production. Large amounts have been spent on land clearing and settlement, feeder-road construction, irrigation, and rural electrification.

The motivation for these programs is no doubt partly political. The Chinese dominate business activity while the Malays are mainly farmers and also control the government. A pro-Malay policy thus tends to be a proagriculture policy. Other countries that have been favorable to and successful in agriculture are South Korea and Thailand. One could say, of course, that these six countries have had relatively high growth rates and so could afford to devote resources to agriculture. But attention to, and success in, agriculture may also be one reason for the high growth rates.

China should also be included in the list of proagriculture countries. Mao, who began as a peasant leader, always counted on the rural population as his main political base. The tilt of policy toward agriculture has if anything increased since his death, with sizable increases in official prices for major crops and increased latitude for peasants to grow and sell additional produce at market prices.

In addition to these clear success cases, we should note several countries whose policies have been moderately favorable toward agriculture, or at least not markedly unfavorable. This group includes India, Sri Lanka, Pakistan, Egypt, Philippines, and Kenya. There are also several cases of "latter-day conversion," that is, countries that neglected agriculture before the mid-1970s but have now shifted to stimulative policies. In Brazil, for example, agricultural policy was until recently neglectful or actually exploitative. Export taxes, an overvalued exchange rate, and price ceilings on domestic food products had an adverse affect on farm income. The military regime that took power in 1964 shifted policy in a favorable direction. Agriculture benefited from abolition of export taxes, adoption of a floating exchange rate, and lifting of food-price ceilings. There was also a marked increase in rural credit facilities. The real value of loans increased six times between 1960 and 1975. These policies must be partly responsible for the 5 percent growth rate of agricultural output since 1960.

In Burma, there was a marked policy shift around 1975. A "package program" was introduced for rice that included dissemination of high-yield varieties, increased supplies of fertilizer at a subsidized price, and a doubling of the government purchase price. Controls over private sales to the free market were also relaxed. The program produced a rise of 40 percent in rice output within a few years, and this success led to its being extended to groundnuts, maize, wheat, sesame, cotton, beans, and pulses, most of which have also shown substantial increases in yields and output.

In Indonesia, the Suharto regime after 1966 introduced a "rice intensification program," which by 1979 covered about five million hectares. Between 1968 and 1979 rice yields per hectare rose by 40 percent, and rice output by 53 percent. Food output as a whole grew during the 1970s at 3.6 percent per year, compared with a rate of only 1.7 percent from 1953 to 1966.

These examples suggest that agriculture, far from being an inherently laggard sector, is quite responsive to well-conceived government programs.

### TRADE AND EXCHANGE POLICIES

Because of their small economic size, most third-world countries are heavily dependent on foreign trade. This dependence is not forced on them by the more-developed countries. It is inherent in the fact of small output and small purchasing power.

Writers on international economics usually distinguish between "outward-looking" and "inward-looking" trade and exchange policies. The main features of an outward-looking policy are: a realistic and flexible exchange rate; a free market for foreign exchange, rather than government-determined allocations; and efforts to promote exports, including in time exports of manufactured products. The term *outward-looking* connotes a favorable view of trade possibilities and reliance on a growing flow of exports to earn the foreign exchange needed for domestic development.

Inward-looking policies are the opposite of those just described: a fixed exchange rate, which usually becomes increasingly overvalued as a result of domestic inflation; a consequent "scarcity" of foreign exchange, which is then allocated among claimants by a government agency; high and often indiscriminate protection of manufacturing industries, by quantitative restrictions on imports as well as tariff rates, with a view to speeding up import substitution in manufactures;

and a pessimistic view of exports, which are neglected or even penalized through export taxes and the exchange-rate system. This policy package tends to produce sluggish growth of exports, which is then used to justify continuation of the restrictive policies.

The difference between the two is not a simple black-and-white contrast. Both policy sets are matters of *degree*. Inward-looking policies may be highly restrictive or only moderately so. Further, there are protariff as well as antitariff arguments. All the developed countries except Britain were quite protectionist while building up their own industries, and so doctrinaire preaching of free trade to currently developing countries has a hollow ring. The size of the economy makes considerable difference. Strong emphasis on import substitution makes more sense for India or Brazil than for Ivory Coast or Peru.

The fact remains that expert opinion is generally critical of highly inward-looking or import-substituting policies. The adverse effects, of course, vary with the severity of the restrictions imposed and with the stage of industrialization. They apply most strongly after "easy import substitution" in nondurable consumer goods is largely completed and the issue is how rapidly to move into consumer durables, chemicals, metals, machinery, and transport equipment. The adverse effects are usually stressed as follows.

1. The overvalued exchange rate, a hallmark of inward-looking policy, taxes exporters and discourages exports. Because there is excess demand for foreign exchange at the official rate, exchange rationing becomes necessary, and those who receive allocations of exchange get a windfall profit. The antiexport bias usually means also an antiagriculture bias, even when the country has comparative advantage in one or more agricultural goods. This discourages agricultural production. Thus apart from any limitations of foreign demand, export expansion may be slowed from the supply side. Export pessimism, which was urged as a reason for import substitution, can readily become self-fulfilling.
2. A common defect is that protection and other incentives are provided not to a limited number of the most promising "infants" but to any and all branches of manufacturing. Studies of Argentina in the Perón era, for example, show little relation between indicators of comparative advantage for a particular industry and the degree of government support it received. Similar results have been reported by Krueger for Turkey, by Lewis and others for Pakistan, and by Bhagwati and Srinivasan for India. At the extreme, one finds cases of "negative value added"—that is, cases in which the value of inputs exceeds that of outputs when both are valued at world prices. It appears also that the cost of the resources used to save a dollar of foreign exchange by import substitution is often well above the cost of using the same resources to earn a dollar of foreign exchange in export production.
3. Foreign competition is stifled. In some countries a product is put on the "prohibited" list as soon as a domestic source of supply has been created. The

domestic monopolies or oligopolies thus created have no incentive to efficiency, and comparative international studies often show that their unit costs are far out of line with those of foreign sources of supply.

4. The way in which foreign-exchange allocation systems are operated tends to produce additional inefficiency. Very common is the "fair shares" principle, in which foreign exchange to buy imported inputs is allocated among firms in an industry in proportion to their installed capacity. This protects firms already established in an industry against newcomers who might be more efficient. It also encourages overbuilding of capacity to obtain larger quotas, and everybody ends up producing below capacity for lack of inputs. This phenomenon helps to explain the paradox that, in countries where capital is supposedly scarce, industrial capital is often seriously underutilized.

5. Systems of quantitative controls, operated by bureaucracies ranging from moderately efficient to quite inefficient, involve uncertainty, delay, excessive paperwork, bribery, and other economic costs. They also tend to favor large producers with good connections over small and unknown producers, regardless of relative efficiency. Thus government's verbal encouragement to small business is negated in practice by the difficulty of finding one's way through the maze of government controls.

6. The supposed aim of reducing import dependence is not necessarily accomplished by inward-looking policies. Some manufacturing industries, especially of the "finishing touches" type, are heavily dependent on imported inputs. So a crash program of import substitution may in the first instance raise import requirements rather than lower them. Even the objective of raising the growth rate of manufacturing output may not be accomplished. Krueger's study of Turkey concluded that a different, balanced strategy with no antiexport bias would have *raised* the manufacturing growth rate by about one-third. It would also have helped the balance of payments by producing more exports and requiring fewer imports than the policies actually followed.

We should not suppose that third-world governments are blind to these problems or that they cannot learn from experience. Some countries in our sample never embarked on highly restrictive trade policies, preferring a generally outward-looking stance. Ivory Coast, Malaysia, and Thailand are prominent examples. In quite a few others there has been a marked shift in policy over time. The doctrine and practice of import substitution peaked in the 1950s. From 1960 onward, one country after another moved in a liberalizing direction. This evolution of policy is important enough to warrant citing a few examples.

A new policy package was introduced around 1961 in Taiwan and around 1965 in South Korea. The main steps taken were: (1) a substantial currency devaluation and substitution of a unified for a multiple exchange rate; (2) liberalization of import quotas and reduction of tariff rates; and (3) a variety of export incentives, with special attention to exports of manufactures. In Taiwan, for example, these incentives included creation of duty-free processing zones; rebate of customs duties and indirect taxes on imported inputs for export products; reduction of the corporate income tax on export earnings; loans at low interest rates; export insurance; a government institute for market research; and a direct subsidy to some industries, administered through manufacturers' associations.

Taiwan's economic success, of course, has been due to a number of factors, including land reform and progressive agricultural policies. But the shift to outward-looking trade policies has certainly contributed. The response of industrialists to the new policies was strong and rapid. Manufacturing output, exports, and productivity rose at spectacular rates after 1960. Manufactures rapidly came to dominate the export list, replacing primary products, which maintained their volume but fell in percentage terms, a process usually termed "export substitution." The same sequence of events occurred in South Korea after 1965. Hong Kong and Singapore since its separation from Malaysia are also quite open economies. It is striking that, as of 1980, about half of all exports of manufactures from the third world came from this Far Eastern "gang of four."

In the late 1960s Brazil and Colombia moved toward more export-oriented policies. The Colombia policy package included a tax rebate system, refund of import duties on inputs, credit at a low rate of interest (usually slightly negative in real terms), and a movable exchange rate system under which the rate was devalued frequently to reflect differential movement of foreign and domestic prices. In Chile, after replacement of the Allende regime in 1973, there was a wholesale removal of price controls and other government controls over the economy. Tariff and nontariff barriers to imports were reduced dramatically. The exchange rate was massively devalued in 1973, with frequent downward adjustments after that, and exchange controls were eliminated. Under the new regime GDP grew rapidly in the late 1970s, exports rose from 40 percent to 50 percent of GDP, and nontraditional exports did particularly well, with copper falling below half of all exports for the first time.

Pakistan liberalized trade somewhat in the early 1960s, then slid back, then returned to a proexport stance in the mid-1970s. Exports, which had been growing at less than 2 percent a year, grew from 1976 to 1980 at 15.3 percent per year. By 1980 finished manufactures were half of all exports, semimanufactures 30 percent, and primary products only 20 percent. Egypt, after the "opening to the West" in 1974, adopted more liberal policies as regards both foreign trade and private investment. The export/GDP ratio rose from about 14 percent in 1970 to 34 percent in 1980, partly but not entirely due to rising oil revenues. There was a general liberalization of economic policies in Sri Lanka in 1978, when a conservative government was installed after a long period of socialist rule. The new policies included exchange-rate unification and devaluation and a liberalization of import controls. Turkey launched a reform program in January 1980 designed to move toward greater reliance on market forces as against quantitative controls and a more outward-looking policy stance.

Since 1960, in short, the trend has been away from extreme import substitution and toward greater integration into the world economy along lines of comparative advantage. A policy shift in this direction has typically led to a sharp spurt in export growth. Meanwhile countries that have clung to inward-looking policies have experienced slow export growth and a shrinking share of world markets.

### PUBLIC OPERATION OF INDUSTRY

In the developed countries railroads, electric power systems, and other public utilities are normally government-owned, though the United States is an exception in this respect. Other sectors are predominantly under private ownership, though there is some government ownership of manufacturing in Britain and France and rather more in Italy. Government enterprises are normally organized as semi-autonomous public corporations whose managers are not subject to day-to-day political intervention by government. They are expected to operate on business principles and to earn enough so that they do not become a burden on the general budget.

In third-world countries, too, government ownership of public utilities is virtually universal. But many governments have gone beyond this into agricultural marketing, banking, mining, and manufacturing. Even in countries with a predominantly capitalist orientation, government is usually the main investment banker. In Brazil, for example, government banks are estimated to provide 70 percent of all investment funds. In a number of countries government has also taken over the commercial banking system. Oil and mineral enterprises are usually government-owned. The historical reason is that before 1940 these enterprises were almost all owned by private foreign companies. Nationalizing them thus seemed the most direct way of asserting the country's control over its natural resources and also of appropriating the large profit streams these enterprises usually yield.

One indicator of the importance of state-owned enterprises in the economy is their investment as a percentage of gross fixed capital formation. In the late 1970s this was 23 percent in Brazil and 23 percent in South Korea, countries with a generally private-enterprise orientation. But it was 33 percent in India, 45 percent in Pakistan, 61 percent in Burma and Zambia, and 68 percent in Algeria.*

The main concern here is with manufacturing, in which practice varies most from country to country and the merit of public ownership is perhaps most debatable. In most countries of our sample the government-owned share of value added in manufacturing is below 20 percent, and often below 10 percent. But it is about 20 percent in India, 25 percent in Ivory Coast, 30 percent in Mexico and Turkey; and it reaches 40 percent in Tanzania, 50 percent in Algeria, 55 percent in Burma, 65 percent in Egypt, and 70 percent in Iraq.

*World Development Report, 1983* (Washington: IBRD, 1983), p. 49.

In a dozen or so countries, then, state enterprises and private concerns share the manufacturing sector. The division is to some extent along product lines, with government tending to dominate in capital goods and intermediates while consumer-goods production is mainly in private hands. The government enterprises are relatively few in number but large in scale. Private enterprises are larger in number but much smaller in average scale. They are also more labor-intensive, and their share of manufacturing employment is well above their share of output. Private businesses are at some disadvantage relative to state enterprises with regard to allocations of credit, foreign exchange, and material inputs. Despite this, the private sector has managed to survive and in some countries shows surprising vigor. The public-private percentages are thus not frozen forever but may be expected to change in response to the evolution of market demand and shifts in public policy.

A number of country studies have tried to appraise the economic performance of state economic enterprises. Several possible criteria are available. Profit performance alone is not conclusive, because marginal-cost pricing may sometimes be socially efficient and may involve financial loss. But when one sees most enterprises losing money most of the time, one is bound to have doubts. In some cases private and state enterprises operate side by side in the same industry, which means that comparative appraisal is possible. It is relevant also to compare unit costs and prices of state enterprises with world price levels, and with unit costs of comparable plants in other countries.

The evidence is somewhat mixed. In South Korea and Ivory Coast, for example, there are some government manufacturing enterprises that seem to operate with reasonable efficiency. These are labor-scarce economies in which there is no incentive for overstaffing; and their governments are stable, pragmatic, and outward-looking. In many other countries, however, observers judge the efficiency of state enterprises to be relatively low. A few examples may be cited.

In India, the private rate of return in public-sector industries is typically low, though this sometimes results from deliberate underpricing, which may have an economic rationale. The social rate of return also appears to be low and declining. Assuming a shadow wage of 60 percent of the market wage, Lal estimates that the average social rate of return to Indian manufacturing in 1968 was 5.4 percent. If the shadow wage is assumed equal to the market wage, the social rate of return drops to −6.1 percent. Bhagwati and Desai are also critical of public-sector performance. Major projects have been launched without a cost-benefit analysis and, where such an analysis was made, government often went ahead with the project despite a low estimated rate of return. So long as the proposed output contributed to some physical target in the five-year plan, all else was forgiven. Long delays in plant completion and serious inflation of costs have been common. Current management has suffered from a variety of ills: use of unqualified generalists from the Indian civil service as top administrators; shortages of technical personnel, due partly to salary scales not competitive with private industry; political heckling of administrators, leading to cautious management and lack of innovation; political decision-making on plant location; and union pressure through political channels for overstaffing and overpayment.

In Egypt, observers judge the management of public enterprises to be quite inefficient, partly because of the top-heavy Egyptian bureaucracy. Despite a large expansion of university capacity since 1952, government has maintained its guarantee of a government job for every university graduate. The result is heavy overstaffing in all government operations. Hansen and Marzouk note that in the large textile industry the government enterprises, which have about three-quarters of total employment, are notably inefficient relative to privately owned plants. The ratio of administrative and service employees to actual operatives is 60 percent in the public sector, 20 percent in the private sector. And government wage scales are more than twice as high.

In Iraq, where government has more than 70 percent of industrial employment, the difficulties of industrial management have been severe. There are several levels of bureaucracy above the producing enterprise. There is high turnover of personnel, extending all the way up to cabinet ministers. Many enterprise directors are army officers with little industrial experience. Workers cannot be laid off, and overstaffing is large. So government's heavy investment of oil revenue in manufacturing has yielded disproportionately small returns.

In Tanzania, the evidence of efficiency of public manufacturing enterprises is conflicting. Clark reports their average profit rate in the early 1970s as 13 percent. On the other hand, they were able to finance only about one-quarter of their new investment. More than half of their new capital came from foreign borrowings, and the remainder from government allocations. A World Bank study reports that man-hour output in government manufacturing is only 70 percent as high as that in comparable private enterprises. This suggests that there may be serious overstaffing in government enterprises.

There is similar evidence from Turkey, Zambia, and other countries. The weight of the evidence suggests that the difficulties of government manufacturing enterprises are built in rather than accidental. They result from a combination of too many levels of bureaucracy above the enterprise, poor selection of and inadequate rewards for industrial managers, and failure to shield the enterprise against day-to-day political intervention. Such intervention is pervasive, including pressure for underpricing, for unduly high wage scales, for hiring of unnecessary workers or prohibition of layoffs, for appointment of managers on the basis of connections rather than qualifications. Most serious is the lack of a budget constraint, since deficits can always be made up from the government budget. Enterprise revenues often fail even to cover operating costs, including depreciation allowances, and constitute a continuing drain on the treasury. An IMF study of 64 public corporations in all parts of the world found that, after providing for depreciation, they had on average a net operating *loss* equal to 8 percent of revenue.

This operating deficit, plus all net investment, had to be covered by outside funds, of which about half came from the general government budget.*

A negative verdict on public enterprise does not suggest any immediate remedy. Disillusionment has certainly set in in some countries, and a good deal of rethinking is going on. Selling off public manufacturing concerns to private investors is often not a viable political option, though it has been done on occasion. What government usually could do is to slow down or stop expansion of the public manufacturing sector and leave future increments in capacity largely to private concerns. Thus a 50 percent government share of manufacturing today could readily shrink to 25 percent over two or three decades. Some countries seem presently to be moving in this direction, and others may do so in future.

Private producers, of course, are not necessarily efficient either. Efficiency depends partly on how far they are exposed to the chastening effect of competition. So the argument for privatization is strongest for large economies and for industries of relatively small optimum scale. Even a private monopolist, however, faces a budget constraint; and increases in efficiency are profitable even if not essential.

OTHER TYPES OF MARKET INTERVENTION

In addition to the policy areas already considered, many third-world governments intervene heavily in the pricing of commodities and factors of production. It would be charitable to attribute this to sophisticated reasoning about market failure and the need for offsetting action by government. But it probably stems mainly from political pressures, which operate also in the richer countries. People want larger incomes and lower prices, and any government that depends at all on public favor is likely to respond. I shall comment briefly on consumer-goods pricing, industrial licensing systems, interest-rate policy, and wage policy.

1. *Pricing.* Subsidized pricing of consumer goods is widespread, especially for basic foodstuffs such as rice, wheat, and bread, for passenger transport and other public-utility services, and recently for petroleum products. This distorts demand patterns. In some countries subsidized bread is the cheapest form of animal food and is so used. The subsidies are a heavy drain on the government budget, making it difficult to finance current services and infrastructure development. And the controls are usually evaded to some extent. In Ghana and in Uganda under Amin, attempts at universal price control led to universal evasion, with actual transactions conducted in unofficial or "parallel" markets.

Subsidies are usually justified as a way of protecting the real income of the poorest groups in the population. But the subsidized price is available to everyone, regardless of income level. In recognition of this, the new conservative government of Sri Lanka drastically reduced the long-standing rice subsidy while at the

*Andrew H. Gault and Guiseppe Dutlo, "Financial Performance of Government-Owned Corporations in Less Developed Countries," *IMF Staff Papers*, March 1968, pp. 102–42.

same time introducing a United States–type food-stamp system applying only to those below a certain income level. Some countries, too, have had the political courage to raise rail and bus fares and other public-utility prices to levels bearing some realistic relation to production costs. Courage is indeed required, for even in such tightly controlled countries as Poland any effort to raise prices toward market-clearing levels can lead to street riots.

2. *Licensing*. In many African and Asian countries, any new industrial enterprise must apply for a government license. Some branches of industry may be reserved for the public sector. But even within the private sector it is argued that investment decisions should conform to an overall national plan. The difficulties arising from such a system, especially well documented in the case of India, are similar to those noted earlier for exchange-allocation systems: uncertainty and delay, the temptation to speed things up or bend the rules through bribery, stifling of initiative, barring of new competitors, a bias toward large as against small producers. The idea that governments know better than private individuals how to use capital effectively was roundly denounced by Adam Smith. His critique of European government decisions in the eighteenth century seems at least equally applicable to third-world governments in the late twentieth century.

3. *Interest Rates*. Interest rates, like controlled consumer prices, have been afflicted by a tendency toward underpricing. Interest-rate ceilings are often so low as to result in a negative real rate. This naturally leads to large excess demand and the allocation of loans, instead of being guided by which projects can afford to pay the market rate, is determined by bank officials whose decisions are bound to be somewhat arbitrary. Low interest rates combined with imported capital goods, which are made artificially cheap by low duties, overvalued exchange rates, and other policies, also produce a capital-intensive bias in investment projects. It is notorious that the manufacturing sectors of third-world countries often create little employment and fail to make effective use of the ample labor supply. This is due partly to underpricing of capital and (as we shall see) overpricing of labor. Low interest rates also discourage private saving, making it harder to raise the national savings rate to an adequate level. Countries that have raised interest rates sharply to reflect the real scarcity of capital in the economy, as South Korea did in the mid-1960s, have been rewarded by a marked increase in saving as well as more effective utilization of capital.

4. *Wages*. In many third-world economies one observes a marked rise of real wages in "modern-sector" activities and a growing rural-urban income gap. This occurs even in the face of ample labor supplies and growing open unemployment. Private employers often raise wages voluntarily, partly to attract and stabilize a labor force of good quality and perhaps also because it seems inequitable that the much higher productivity of labor in "modern" than in traditional activities should be reflected entirely in profit, as it is in the Lewis model. But government often forces the pace through minimum-wage laws and through generous wage scales for government employees. Especially in Africa, government employees

often form one-third to one-half of the modern-sector labor force; and government, under political pressure to be a "good employer," tends to serve as wage leader for the private economy.

Whatever the mechanism, the result is often a wage scale for modern-sector employees well above any market-clearing level. This encourages substitution of capital for labor in industry, thus reducing employment opportunities. At the same time the growing urban-rural income gap stimulates heavy migration, which overcrowds the cities and intensifies both open and concealed unemployment.

The list of possible price distortions is thus a long one. Factor prices are distorted by interest-rate and wage policies. Product prices are distorted by exchange-rate policy, trade restrictions, farm price ceilings, consumer subsidies, and underpricing of power, transport, and other services. The circumstances responsible for each distortion are different, but their effect is cumulative and can be seriously adverse to economic efficiency and growth.

Researchers at the World Bank have estimated an "index of price distortion" for each of 30 countries based on ratings by country specialists.* The countries in our sample with least price distortion were Thailand, South Korea, Malaysia, Philippines, Kenya, and Colombia (Taiwan, no longer included in IBRD tables, would probably also fall in this group). The countries with largest price distortions were Pakistan, Peru, Argentina, Chile, Tanzania, Nigeria, and Ghana.

It is interesting that the average 1970–80 performance of the low-distortion group was superior to that of the high-distortion group in important respects: annual GDP growth rate (6.8 percent *versus* 3.1 percent); domestic savings/income ratio (21.4 percent *versus* 13.8 percent); additional output per unit of investment (27.6 percent *versus* 16.8 percent); and annual growth rate of export volume (6.7 percent *versus* 0.7 percent). Although no simple causal relation can be inferred from these data, the association of market-directed prices and good economic performance seems significant.

CAPITALISM, SOCIALISM, AND ALL THAT

The pure capitalist economy is an abstraction; we shall never see such a thing in reality. Even in the nineteenth century, Europe and North America deviated significantly from the capitalist pattern, and these deviations have increased in the twentieth century. So we speak now of the "mixed economy," an ambiguous term in that the mix of private initiative and government intervention varies considerably from country to country. Broadly, we mean an economy that relies mainly on private ownership of productive assets and on private economic deci-

---

*The technique was to rate each type of distortion in a particular country as low, medium, or high and to assign numerical values of 1 for low, 2 for medium, and 3 for high. An overall average was then computed for the country. The averages range from 1.14 in Malawi and 1.43 in Thailand to 2.71 in Nigeria and 2.86 in Ghana. *World Development Report, 1983* (Washington, DC: IBRD, 1983), pp. 57–63.

sions coordinated mainly through a network of markets and prices. But along with this goes a substantial output of public goods, government ownership of public utilities and sometimes of other industries, government programs aimed at redistributing income, a tax system that collects a substantial percentage of national income, and a variety of government regulations over the private economy.

Of the 34 countries in our sample that have managed to achieve intensive growth, 22 clearly are mixed economies in this sense. The mix varies, just as it does in more-developed countries. Pakistan, Taiwan, Malaysia, and Thailand are more wholeheartedly committed to private ownership than are Turkey, Iran, or Indonesia. Kenya, Ivory Coast, and Nigeria have a stronger private-enterprise orientation than Ghana or Morocco. Argentina, Colombia, and Venezuela are somewhat more capitalist than Mexico or Brazil.

Seven countries profess a socialist orientation. These are Tanzania, Zambia, Algeria, Egypt, Iraq, India, and Burma. These economies are also mixed in that private production is by no means ruled out. It is usually dominant in agriculture, trade, handicrafts, and small-scale manufacturing. But private industry and profit-making are viewed with suspicion, as needing to be kept under careful control. The socialist tilt shows up in an unusually large public sector that encompasses much of large-scale manufacturing, in a propensity to regulate the private economy in great detail, and sometimes in redistributive income policies.

Three countries have changed direction recently and are thus hard to classify. Peru was rather strongly oriented toward private enterprise in the past, but the military regime that took over in 1968 embarked on widespread nationalization of industry. How much of this will last under restored civilian rule remains to be seen. In Uganda, too, the Idi Amin regime confiscated most private industries, though it failed to operate them effectively. The post-Amin economy is still in shambles, and its future structure remains unclear. Sri Lanka would have been classified as socialist in the Indian pattern up to the late 1970s, but the conservative government that has now won two elections has reversed course on many points. We should perhaps add Zimbabwe to the list of uncertain cases. It was strongly capitalist in the past, with much of its industry foreign-owned. The new African prime minister, Robert Mugabe, professes socialism as a goal; but just how, and how rapidly, he will move in this direction is unclear at this date.

This leaves two countries, Cuba and China, in which government is dominated by a communist party and in which virtually all productive assets are state-owned. In other writings* I have explored the economic performance of this type of regime, and nothing need be added here. Suffice it to say that comprehensive socialization, although it is compatible with intensive growth, provides no firm assurance of such growth. China's moderate growth of per capita income puts it in the middle range of third-world countries, well below the star performers but well

*The Three Worlds of Economics (New Haven: Yale University Press, 1971); and Image and Reality in Economic Development (New Haven: Yale University Press, 1977), chap. 15.

above the other Asian giant, India. On the other hand Cuba's economy was badly mismanaged from 1958 through the early 1970s and, though production has since recovered somewhat, per capita income is probably still below the 1960 level. There is little Western literature on North Korea or Vietnam. One has an impression of high growth in North Korea, low or zero growth in Vietnam, not surprising in view of the chronic warfare in which that country has been engaged since 1940.

Returning to the noncommunist countries, one is struck by the degree of ambiguity and internal contradiction in policies toward private business activity. This is most marked in the professedly socialist countries, but it is by no means absent in others. On one hand there is an implicit reliance on private producers to organize resources and raise national output. But on the other hand their efforts are often checkmated by a querulous or hostile government attitude and a maze of government restrictions. Many years ago an office-mate of mine at Harvard, now a distinguished member of the profession, remarked with the air of one discovering an obscure truth, ''You know, capitalists have to be allowed to make money.'' Many third-world governments are reluctant to acknowledge this necessity.

One can well understand suspicion of foreign multinational corporations. It is possible for a country to gain by permitting multinational investment in its territory, but the terms of each deal need to be carefully specified. One wonders, however, whether this suspicion should be extended to indigenous businessmen, who are not really the monsters of Marxist demonology. They are actually rather timid and peaceable creatures who can be tamed to serve the public interest. Instead of repeating Adam Smith's famous paragraph on this point, let me quote Maynard Keynes (1938) in a letter to President Franklin Roosevelt:

> Businessmen have a different set of delusions from politicians; and need, therefore, different handling. They are, however, much milder than politicians, at the same time allured and terrified by the glare of publicity, easily persuaded to be ''patriots,'' perplexed, bemused, even terrified, yet only too anxious to take a cheerful view, vain perhaps but very unsure of themselves, pathetically responsive to a kind word.
>
> You could do anything you liked with them, if you would treat them (even the big ones), not as wolves and tigers, but as domestic animals by nature, even though they have been badly brought up and not trained as you would wish.
>
> It is a mistake to think that they are more immoral than politicians. If you work them into the surly, obstinate, terrified mood, of which domestic animals, wrongly handled, are so capable, the nation's burdens will not get carried to market; and in the end public opinion will veer their way.

We should recall also that Karl Marx, like Adam Smith, considered capitalism a powerful engine for raising productive capacity. Socialism was to take over only after a modern industrial economy had been created. But disciples are rarely as wise as the master. Latter-day Marxists often turn Marx on his head and advocate socialist organization *before* capitalism has had an opportunity to do its constructive work.

"Capitalist" has now become an epithet. It is perhaps difficult for third-world governments to respond to the question "Do you sincerely want to be rich?" by openly espousing capitalism. But perhaps they might do so quietly. They might recall that the most thoroughly capitalist of the developed countries, Japan, also has the strongest growth record. Also, of the 20 third-world countries ranked highest in recent income growth (see table 2), almost all have a clear private-enterprise orientation. Except for Algeria and Iraq, which have kept afloat on a flood of oil revenue, countries with a socialist orientation rank lower in the table.

### LESSONS FROM HISTORY?

Perhaps not *lessons,* but something more in the nature of *suggestions.* An initial suggestion is that we stop using the term *third world.* Whatever purpose it may serve in political debate, it has no economic merit. The third world is simply a group of countries, as diverse as may be, each of which should be viewed independently, just as we view Australia or France.

A second suggestion relates to the sources of long-term growth. In the United Nations Commission on Trade and Development (UNCTAD) and other international bodies it has been fashionable for many of the lower-income countries to blame their problems on the higher-income countries. They are poor because we have exploited them in the past, and they can flourish only if we will finance them in future. This is largely shadow play. The fact that some countries have grown so much faster than others in the same international environment is in itself a convincing refutation. The trade and aid policies of the developed countries doubtless have some impact; and one can make a good case that these countries, by following policies that are *in their own interest,* can also contribute to third-world growth. But when we ask *why* a particular country has grown more or less rapidly, we come back invariably to internal factors: the resource base, the structure of economic institutions, the stability and competence of government, the wisdom of policy measures. In large measure a country grows by internal effort, which outsiders can encourage but not replace.

A third suggestion comes dangerously close to advice to third-world governments, which are likely to be unresponsive to outside advice unless it comes from international bankers. Thirty years ago Arthur Lewis noted a tendency for third-world governments to undertake more than they can accomplish:

> The list of governmental functions . . . is even wider in the less developed than in the more developed economies. . . . On the other hand, the governments of the less developed countries are at the same time less capable of taking on a wide range of functions than are the governments of the more

developed. Their administrations tend to be more corrupt and less efficient, and a smaller part of the national income can be spared for government activity. This is another of the paradoxes of economic growth. Just as poor countries need to save more than rich countries, but cannot afford as much, so also poor countries need more and better government activity than rich ones, but are apt to get less and worse. In fact, one cannot usefully consider in an abstract way what functions a government ought to exercise without taking into account the capabilities of the government in question. It is very easy to overload the governments of less developed economies, and it is quite clear that it is better for them to confine themselves to what they can manage than for them to take on an excessive range.*

Experience since Lewis wrote underscores the wisdom of his comment. Most third-world governments are trying to do too much with too little. The range of their administrative controls over the economy is wider than in the developed countries, while at the same time their civil-service staffs are weaker. The common result, in addition to confusion, delay, and waste, is that the paper controls are not enforced effectively and do not have the intended effect. In the worst cases, such as Uganda, Ghana, and Zaire, the control system dissolves in a welter of smuggling, bribery, and evasion. There is need for a clearer recognition that administrative capacity is a scarce resource, which can be enlarged only gradually and which meanwhile needs to be husbanded and focused on high-priority objectives. The best government decision is often a decision to do nothing.

Governments might well restrain their urge to control everything in the economy and consider the advantages of greater reliance on private initiative. The payoff to private initiative is especially large in agriculture, to which most governments pay less attention than they should. But it is large also in trade, road transport, service industries, and manufacturing. The gradual growth of an industrial and commercial middle class, which was the essence of nineteenth-century development, still has much to contribute in the twentieth century and beyond.

*W. Arthur Lewis, *The Theory of Economic Growth* (Homewood, IL: Richard D. Irwin, 1955), p. 382.

# Bibliography

GENERAL ECONOMIC STUDIES

## Economic Growth

Balassa, Bela. *The Newly Industrializing Countries in the World Economy*. New York: Pergamon Press, 1981.

Baran, Paul. *The Political Economy of Growth*. New York: Monthly Review Press, 1957.

Birnberg, Thomas B., and Resnick, Stephen A. *Colonial Development: An Econometric Study*. New Haven: Yale University Press, 1975.

Boserup, Ester. *The Conditions of Agricultural Growth*. Chicago: Aldine Publishing Company, 1964.

———. *Population and Technological Change: A Study of Long-Term Trends*. Chicago: University of Chicago Press, 1981.

Chenery, Hollis. "Patterns of Industrial Growth." *American Economic Review* 50 (September 1960):624–54.

———. *Structural Change and Development Policy*. Oxford: Oxford University Press for the World Bank, 1979.

Chenery, Hollis, and Ahluwalia, Montek S. *Redistribution with Growth*. Oxford: Oxford University Press for the World Bank, 1974.

Chenery, Hollis, and Syrquin, Moises. *Patterns of Development, 1950–1970*. Oxford: Oxford University Press for the World Bank, 1975.

Clark, Colin, *The Conditions of Economic Progress*. London: Macmillan, 1951.

Cohen, Benjamin J. *The Question of Imperialism: The Political Economy of Dominance and Dependence*. New York: Basic Books, 1973.

Fei, John C. H., and Ranis, Gustav. *Development of the Labor-Surplus Economy: Theory and Policy*. Homewood, IL: Richard D. Irwin, 1964.

Gerschenkron, Alexander. *Economic Backwardness in Historical Perspective*. Cambridge: Harvard University Press, 1962.

Gould, J. D. *Economic Growth in History*. London: Methuen, 1972.

130

Guha, Ashok S. *An Evolutionary View of Economic Growth.* Oxford: Oxford University Press, 1981.

Hicks, John R. *Essays in World Economics.* Oxford: Clarendon Press, 1959.

Hoffman, Walther. *The Growth of Industrial Economies.* Manchester: University of Manchester Press, 1958.

Hoselitz, Bert F., ed. *The Role of Small Industry in the Process of Economic Growth.* The Hague: Mouton, 1968.

International Bank for Reconstruction and Development. *World Development Report.* Washington DC: IBRD, 1982, 1983.

Ishikawa, Shigeru. *Economic Development in Asian Perspectives.* Tokyo: Kinokuniya Bookstore, 1967.

————. *Essays on Technology, Employment and Institutions in Economic Development: Comparative Asian Experience.* Tokyo: Kinokuniya Bookstore, 1981.

Johnson, Harry G. *On Economics and Society.* Chicago: University of Chicago Press, 1975.

Johnson, John J., ed. *The Role of the Military in Underdeveloped Countries.* Princeton: Princeton University Press, 1962.

Johnston, Bruce, and Kilby, Peter. *Agriculture and Structural Transformation: Economic Strategies in Late-developing Countries.* Oxford: Oxford University Press, 1975.

Keynes, John Maynard. Letter to President Franklin D. Roosevelt, February 1938. Roosevelt Library, Hyde Park, NY. Reported in the *New York Times,* May 24, 1983, p. F6.

Krueger, Anne O., et al. *Trade and Employment in Developing Countries.* Chicago: University of Chicago Press, 1981.

Kumar, Joginder. *Population and Land in World Agriculture.* Population Monograph Series, no. 12. Berkeley: University of California Press for Institute of International Studies, 1973.

Kuznets, Simon. "International Differences in Capital Formation and Financing." In *Capital Formation and Economic Growth,* ed. Moses Abramovitz. New York: National Bureau of Economic Research, 1956.

————. "Quantitative Aspects of the Economic Growth of Nations: Capital Formation Proportions." *Economic Development and Cultural Change* 8 (July 1960a): 1–96.

————. *Six Lectures on Economic Growth.* IL: Free Press of Glencoe, 1960b.

————. *Modern Economic Growth: Rate, Structure, and Spread.* New Haven: Yale University Press, 1966.

————. *Economic Growth of Nations: Total Output and Production Structure.* Cambridge: Harvard University Press, 1971.

————. "Problems in Comparing Recent Growth Rates for Developed and Less Developed Countries." *Economic Development and Cultural Change* 20 (January 1972):185–209.

Kuznets, Simon; Moore, W. E.; and Spengler, J. J.; eds. *Economic Growth: Brazil, India, Japan.* Durham, NC: Duke University Press, 1955.

Lewis, W. Arthur. "Economic Development with Unlimited Supplies of La-
  bour." *Manchester School* 22 (May 1954):139–91.
———. *The Theory of Economic Growth*. Homewood, IL: Richard D. Irwin,
  1955.
———. "The Slowing Down of the Engine of Growth." *American Economic
  Review* 70 (September 1980):555–64.
Little, Ian M. D. *Economic Development: Theory, Policy and International Rela-
  tions*. New York: Basic Books, 1982.
Maddison, Angus. *Phases of Capitalist Development*. Oxford: Oxford University
  Press, 1982.
Malinvaud, Edmond, ed. *Economic Growth and Resources*. Proceedings of the
  Fifth World Congress of the International Economic Association. New York:
  St. Martin's Press, 1979.
Mill, John Stuart. *Principles of Political Economy*. London: Routledge and Kee-
  gan Paul, 1965 [1848].
Mitchell, Brian. *International Historical Statistics: Africa and Asia*. New York:
  New York University Press, 1982.
Myint, Hla. *The Economics of the Developing Countries*. London: Hutchinson,
  1964.
Myrdal, Gunnar. *Economic Theory and Underdeveloped Regions*. London:
  G. Duckworth, 1957.
———. *Asian Drama: An Inquiry into the Poverty of Nations*. New York: Pan-
  theon, 1968.
Paauw, Douglas S., and Fei, John C. H. *The Transition in Open Dualistic Econo-
  mies: Theory and Southeast Asian Experiences*. New Haven: Yale University
  Press, 1973.
Ranis, Gustav, ed. *Government and Economic Development*. New Haven: Yale
  University Press, 1971.
Ranis, Gustav, et al., eds. *Comparative Development Perspectives*. Boulder, CO:
  Westview Press, 1983.
Resnick, Stephen. "The Decline of Rural Industry under Export Expansion."
  *Journal of Economic History* 30, 1 (March 1970):51–73.
Reynolds, Lloyd G. *The Three Worlds of Economics*. New Haven: Yale Univer-
  sity Press, 1971.
———, ed. *Agriculture in Development Theory*. New Haven: Yale University
  Press, 1975.
———. *Image and Reality in Economic Development*. New Haven: Yale Univer-
  sity Press, 1977.
Rosenstein-Rodan, Paul. "International Aid to Underdeveloped Countries." *Re-
  view of Economics and Statistics* 43 (May 1961):107–38.
Rostow, Walt W. "The Take-off into Self-sustained Growth." *Economic Journal*
  66 (March 1956):25–48.
———. *The World Economy: History and Prospect*. Austin: University of Texas
  Press, 1978.

Schultz, T. W. *Transforming Traditional Agriculture.* New Haven: Yale University Press, 1964.

Smith, Adam. *An Inquiry into the Nature and Causes of the Wealth of Nations.* Homewood, IL: Richard D. Irwin, 1963 [1776].

Stolper, Wolfgang. *Planning without Facts: Lessons in Resource Allocation for Nigeria's Development.* Cambridge: Harvard University Press, 1966.

Summers, Robert; Kravis, Irving B.; and Heston, Alan. "International Comparison of Real Product and Its Composition: 1950–77." *Review of Income and Wealth,* ser. 26, no. 1, March 1980, pp. 19–66.

Wallerstein, Immanuel. *The Capitalist World Economy.* Cambridge and New York: Cambridge University Press, 1979.

Winks, Robin W., ed. *British Imperialism: God, Gold and Glory.* Holt, Rinehart and Winston, 1973.

## The International Economy

Ashworth, William. *A Short History of the International Economy, 1850–1950.* London: Longmans Green, 1952.

Bairoch, Paul. *The Economic Development of the Third World since 1900.* Berkeley: University of California Press, 1975.

Bhagwati, Jagdish N. "The Theory of Comparative Advantage in the Context of Underdevelopment and Growth." *Pakistan Development Review,* Autumn 1962.

———. *Anatomy and Consequences of Exchange Control Regimes.* Cambridge, MA: Ballinger, 1978.

Chenery, Hollis. "Comparative Advantage and Development Policy." *American Economic Review* 50, 1 (March 1961):18–51.

Fieldhouse, D. K. *Economics and Empire, 1830–1914.* London: Weidenfeld and Nicholson, 1973.

Kenwood, A. G., and Lougheed, A. L. *The Growth of the International Economy, 1820–1960.* London: Allen and Unwin, 1975.

Kindleberger, Charles P. *Government and International Trade.* Essays in International Finance, no. 129. Princeton, NJ: Department of Economics, Princeton University, 1978.

Kuznets, Simon. "Quantitative Aspects of the Economic Growth of Nations: X. Level and Structure of Foreign Trade: Long-Term Trends." *Economic Development and Cultural Change* 15, 2, Part II (January 1967):1–14.

Latham, A. J. H. *The International Economy and the Underdeveloped World, 1865–1914.* Totowa, NJ: Rowman and Littlefield, 1978.

Lewis, W. Arthur. *Aspects of Tropical Trade, 1883–1965.* Stockholm: Almqvist and Wiksell, 1969.

———, ed. *Tropical Development, 1880–1913: Studies in Economic Progress.* London: Allen and Unwin, 1970.

————. *The Evolution of the International Economic Order*. Princeton: Princeton University Press, 1978a.

————. *Growth and Fluctuations, 1870–1913*. London and Boston: Allen and Unwin, 1978b.

Maizels, Alfred. *Industrial Growth and World Trade*. London: Cambridge University Press, 1963.

————. *Exports and Economic Growth of Developing Countries*. London: Cambridge University Press, 1968.

Myint, Hla. "The 'Classical Theory' of International Trade and the Under-developed Countries." *Economic Journal*, June 1958, pp. 317–37.


Population


Boserup, Ester. *The Conditions of Agricultural Growth: The Economics of Agrarian Change under Population Pressure*. Chicago: Aldine, 1965.

————. *Population and Technological Change: A Study of Long-Term Trends*. Chicago: University of Chicago Press, 1981.

Durand, J. Dana. *Historical Estimates of World Population: An Evaluation*. Philadelphia: Population Studies Center, University of Pennsylvania, 1974.

Easterlin, Richard A., ed. *Population and Economic Change in Developing Countries: A Conference Report*. Universities–National Bureau Committee for Economic Research, no. 30. Chicago: University of Chicago Press, 1980.

Kuznets, Simon. *Population, Capital and Growth*. New York: Norton, 1973.

McEvedy, Colin, and Jones, Richard. *Atlas of World Population History*. New York: Facts on File, 1978.

*Population Problems*. Proceedings of the American Philosophical Society, vol. III, no. 3. Philadelphia, 1967.

Tilly, Charles, ed. *Historical Studies of Changing Fertility*. Princeton: Princeton University Press, 1978.


European Economic Development


Ashton, T. S., ed. *An Economic History of England*. Vol. 3, *The Eighteenth Century*. New York: Barnes and Noble, 1955.

Bairoch, Paul, and Lévy-Leboyer, Maurice, eds. *Disparities in Economic Development since the Industrial Revolution*. New York: St. Martin's Press, 1981.

Deane, Phyllis, and Cole, W. A. *British Economic Growth, 1688–1959: Trends and Structure*. Cambridge: Cambridge University Press, 1962.

Jones, Eric L. *The European Miracle*. London: Cambridge University Press, 1981.

Kerridge, Eric. *The Agricultural Revolution*. London: Allen and Unwin, 1967.

Milward, Alan S., and Saul, S. B. *The Development of the Economies of Continental Europe, 1850–1914*. Cambridge: Harvard University Press, 1977.

————. *The Economic Development of Continental Europe, 1780–1870*. London: Allen and Unwin, 1979.

Pollard, Sidney. *Peaceful Conquest: The Industrialization of Europe, 1760–1970*. Oxford: Oxford University Press, 1981.

Rich, E. E., and Wilson, C. H., eds. *The Cambridge Economic History of Europe*. Vol. 4, *The Economy of Expanding Europe in the Sixteenth and Seventeenth Centuries*. Cambridge: Cambridge University Press, 1967.

Woodruff, William. *Impact of Western Man: A Study of Europe's Role in the World Economy, 1750–1960*. New York: St. Martin's Press, 1967.

ASIA

### General

Allen, G. C., and Donnithorne, Audrey G. *Western Enterprise in Indonesia and Malaya: A Study in Economic Development*. London: Allen and Unwin, 1957.

Dernberger, Robert F., ed. *China's Development Experience in Comparative Perspective*. Cambridge: Harvard University Press, 1980.

Fisher, Charles, *Southeast Asia: A Social, Economic and Political Geography*. New York: E. P. Dutton, 1964.

Shand, R. T., ed. *Agricultural Development in Asia*. Canberra: Australian National University Press, 1969.

### Burma

Andrus, J. Russell. *Burmese Economic Life*. 1948. Reprint. Stanford: Stanford University Press, 1956.

Furnivall, J. S. *An Introduction to the Political Economy of Burma*. 3rd ed. Rangoon: People's Literature Committee-House, 1957.

Silverstein, Josef. *Burma: Military Rule and the Politics of Stagnation*. Ithaca: Cornell University Press, 1977.

### China

Eckstein, Alexander. *China's Economic Revolution*. London and New York: Cambridge University Press, 1977.

Feuerwerker, Albert. *The Chinese Economy, 1912–1949*. Michigan Papers in Chinese Studies, no. 1. Ann Arbor: University of Michigan, Center for Chinese Studies, 1968.

————. *The Chinese Economy, ca. 1870–1911*. Michigan Papers in Chinese Studies, no. 5. Ann Arbor: University of Michigan, Center for Chinese Studies, 1969.

Liu Ta-Chung and Yeh K'ung Chia. *The Economy of the Chinese Mainland: National Income and Economic Development, 1933–1959*. Princeton: Princeton University Press, 1965.

Perkins, Dwight M. *Agricultural Development in China, 1368–1968*. Chicago: Aldine Press, 1969.

————, ed. *China's Modern Economy in Historical Perspective*. Stanford: Stanford University Press, 1975.

Rawski, Thomas G. *China's Republican Economy: An Introduction*. Discussion Paper no. 1. Toronto: University of Toronto–York University Joint Centre on Modern East Asia, 1978.

Rawski, Thomas G. *Economic Growth and Employment in China*. New York: Oxford University Press for the World Bank, 1979.

————. *China's Transition to Industrialism*. Ann Arbor: University of Michigan Press, 1980.

India

Bhagwati, Jagdish, and Desai, Padma. *India: Planning for Industrialization: Industrialization and Trade Policies since 1951*. London and New York: Oxford University Press for the Development Centre of the Organization for Economic Cooperation and Development, 1970.

Bhagwati, Jagdish, and Srinivasan, T. N. *India (Foreign Trade Regimes and Economic Development)*. New York: National Bureau of Economic Research, distributed by Columbia University Press, 1975.

Cassen, Robert H. *India: Population, Economy, Society*. New York: Holmes and Meier, 1978.

Gadgil, D. R. *The Industrial Evolution of India in Recent Times, 1860–1939*. 5th ed. Bombay: Indian Branch, Oxford University Press, 1971.

Ganguli, B. N., ed. *Readings in Indian Economic History*. Proceedings of the All-India Seminar on Indian Economic History. New York: Asia Publishing House, 1964.

Kumar, Dharma, and Desai, Meghnad. *The Cambridge Economic History of India: Volume 2, c. 1757–1970*. London: Cambridge University Press, 1983.

Lal, Deepak. *The Hindu Equilibrium: Cultural Stability and Economic Stagnation, India 1500 B.C.–1980 A.D.* Oxford: Oxford University Press, 1984.

Maddison, Angus. *Class Structure and Economic Growth: India and Pakistan since the Moghuls*. New York: Norton, 1972.

Mellor, John W. *The New Economics of Growth: Strategy for India and the Developing World*. Ithaca: Cornell University Press, 1976.

Morris, Morris D. *The Emergence of an Industrial Labor Force in India: A Study of the Bombay Cotton Mills, 1854–1947*. Berkeley: University of California Press, 1965.

Mukherjee, M. *National Income of India: Trends and Structure.* Calcutta: Statistical Publishing Society, 1969.

Raychaudhuri, Tapan, and Habib, Irfan, eds. *The Cambridge Economic History of India: Volume I, c. 1200–c. 1750.* New York: Cambridge University Press, 1982.

Thorner, Daniel. *The Shaping of Modern India.* New Delhi: Allied Publishers for the Sameeksha Trust, 1980.

## Indochina

Robequain, Charles. *The Economic Development of French Indo-China.* London and New York: Oxford University Press, 1944.

## Indonesia

Broek, Jan O. *Economic Development of the Netherlands Indies.* New York: International Secretariat, Institute of Pacific Relations, 1942.

Furnivall, J. S. *Netherlands Indies: A Study of Plural Economy.* 1939. Reprint. London and New York: Cambridge University Press, 1967.

Geertz, Clifford. *Agricultural Involution: The Process of Ecological Change in Indonesia.* Berkeley: University of California Press for the Association of Asian Studies, 1963.

## Japan

Allen, George C. *Japan's Economic Recovery.* London and New York: Oxford University Press, 1958.

Emi, Koichi. *Government Fiscal Activity and Economic Growth in Japan, 1868–1960.* Tokyo: Kinokuniya Bookstore, 1963.

Klein, Lawrence, and Ohkawa, Kazushi, eds. *Economic Growth: The Japanese Experience since the Meiji Era.* Homewood, IL: Richard D. Irwin, 1968.

Lockwood, W. W. *The Economic Development of Japan: Growth and Structural Change.* Princeton: Princeton University Press, 1954.

Ohkawa, K. *Differential Structure and Agriculture: Essays on Dualistic Growth.* Tokyo: Kinokuniya Bookstore, 1972.

Ohkawa, Kazushi; Johnston, B. F.; and Kaneda, H.; eds. *Agriculture and Economic Growth: Japan's Experience.* Princeton: Princeton University Press, 1969.

Ohkawa, Kazushi, and Rosovsky, Henry. *Japanese Economic Growth: Trend Acceleration in the Twentieth Century.* Stanford: Stanford University Press, 1973.

Ranis, Gustav. "The Financing of Japanese Economic Development." *Economic History Review* 11, 3 (April 1959):440–54.

Rosovsky, Henry. *Capital Formation in Japan, 1868–1940.* New York: Free Press of Glencoe, 1961.

————, ed. *Industrialization in Two Systems: Essays in Honor of Alexander Gerschenkron.* New York: Wiley, 1966.

Shinohara, Miyohei. *Growth and Cycles in the Japanese Economy.* Tokyo: Kinokuniya Bookstore, 1962.

————. *Structural Change in Japan's Economic Development.* Tokyo: Kinokuniya Bookstore, 1970.

Tsuru, S. "The Take-off in Japan, 1868–1900." In *The Economics of Take-off into Sustained Growth: Proceedings of a Conference Held by the International Economic Association,* ed. W. W. Rostow. New York: St. Martin's Press, 1963.

### Malaysia

Hoffman, Lutz, and Fe, Tan Siew. *Industrial Growth, Employment and Foreign Investment in Peninsular Malaysia.* Kuala Lumpur and New York: Oxford University Press, 1980.

Lim Chong-Yah. *Economic Development of Modern Malaya.* New York and Kuala Lumpur: Oxford University Press, 1967.

Lim, David, ed. *Readings in Malaysian Economic Development.* Kuala Lumpur and New York: Oxford University Press, 1975.

Snodgrass, Donald R. *Inequality and Economic Development in Malaysia.* A Study Sponsored by the Harvard Institute for International Development. New York: Oxford University Press, 1980.

### Pakistan

Falcon, Walter P., and Papanek, Gustav, eds. *Development Policy II—The Pakistan Experience.* Cambridge: Harvard University Press, 1971.

Islam, Nurul. *Foreign Trade and Economic Controls in Development: The Case of United Pakistan.* New Haven: Yale University Press, 1981.

Lewis, Stephen R., Jr. *Economic Policy and Industrial Growth in Pakistan.* Cambridge: M.I.T. Press, 1969.

————. *Pakistan: Industrialization and Trade Policies.* Oxford: Oxford University Press for the Development Centre of the Organization for Economic Cooperation and Development, 1970.

### Philippines

Baldwin, Robert E. *The Philippines (Foreign Trade Regimes and Economic Development).* New York: National Bureau of Economic Research, distributed by Columbia University Press, 1975.

Hooley, R. W. "Long-term Growth of the Philippine Economy, 1902–61." *Philippine Economic Journal,* First Semester, 1968.

Power, John H., and Sicat, Gerardo P. *The Philippines: Industrialization and Trade Policies.* London and New York: Oxford University Press for the Development Centre of the Organization for Economic Cooperation and Development, 1971.

Ranis, Gustav, ed. *Sharing in Development: A Program of Employment, Equity, and Growth for the Philippines.* Geneva: International Labour Organization, 1973.

Valdepenas, Vincente B., Jr., and Bautista, Gemelino M. *The Emergence of the Philippine Economy.* Manila: Papyrus Press, 1977.

## South Korea

Frank, Charles R., Jr.; Kim Kwang Suk; and Westphal, Larry. *South Korea (Foreign Trade Regimes and Economic Development).* New York: National Bureau of Economic Research, distributed by Columbia University Press, 1975.

Kim Kwang Suk and Roemer, Michael. *Growth and Structural Transformation.* Cambridge: Council on East Asian Studies, Harvard University; distributed by Harvard University Press, 1979.

Kuznets, Paul W. *Economic Growth and Structure in the Republic of Korea.* New Haven: Yale University Press, 1977.

## Sri Lanka

Karunatilake, H. N. S. *Economic Development in Ceylon.* New York: Praeger, 1971.

Snodgrass, Donald R. *Ceylon: An Export Economy in Transition.* Homewood, IL: Richard D. Irwin, 1966.

## Taiwan

Fei, J. C. H.; Ranis, Gustav; and Kuo, S. *Growth with Equity: The Taiwan Case.* New York: Oxford University Press for the World Bank, 1979.

Ho, Samuel P. S. *Economic Development of Taiwan, 1860–1970.* New Haven: Yale University Press, 1978.

## Thailand

Ingram, James C. *Economic Change in Thailand, 1850–1970.* Stanford: Stanford University Press, 1971.

Marzouk, G. A. *Economic Development and Policies: Case-Study of Thailand 1952–1970.* Rotterdam: Rotterdam University Press, 1972.

LATIN AMERICA

General

Cortes Conde, Roberto. *The First Stages of Modernization in Spanish America.* New York: Harper and Row, 1974.

Furtado, Celso. *Economic Development of Latin America: A Survey from Colonial Times to the Cuban Revolution.* 2d ed. Cambridge: Cambridge University Press, 1976.

Prebisch, R. *Change and Development: Latin America's Great Task.* Report Submitted to the Inter-American Development Bank. New York: Praeger, 1971.

Sanchez-Albornoz, Nicholás. *The Population of Latin America: A History.* Berkeley: University of California Press, 1974.

Stein, Stanley J., and Stein, Barbara H. *The Colonial Heritage of Latin America.* New York: Oxford University Press, 1970.


Argentina

Diaz Alejandro, Carlos F. *Essays on the Economic History of the Argentine Republic.* New Haven: Yale University Press, 1970.
———. "Not Less Than One Hundred Years of Argentine Economic History." In *Comparative Development Perspectives,* ed. Gustav Ranis et al. Boulder, CO: Westview Press, 1983.


Brazil

Baer, Werner. *The Brazilian Economy: Its Growth and Development.* Columbus: Grid, 1979.

Bergsman, Joel. *Brazil: Industrialization and Trade Policies.* London and New York: Oxford University Press for the Development Centre of the Organization for Economic Cooperation and Development, 1970.

Furtado, Celso. *The Economic Growth of Brazil: A Survey from Colonial to Modern Times.* Berkeley: University of California Press, 1963.

Leff, Nathaniel. *Economic Policy-making and Development in Brazil, 1947–1964.* New York: Wiley, 1968.
———. *Underdevelopment and Development in Brazil.* Vol. 1, *Economic Structure and Change, 1822–1947.* London and Boston: Allen and Unwin, 1982.

Merrick, Thomas W., and Graham, Douglas H. *Population and Economic Development in Brazil: 1800 to the Present.* Baltimore: Johns Hopkins University Press, 1979.

Winpenny, J. T. *Brazil—Manufactured Exports and Government Policy: Brazil's Experience since 1939.* London: Latin American Publications Fund, distributed by Grant and Cutler, 1972.

## Chile

Behrman, Jere R. *Chile (Foreign Trade Regimes and Economic Development)*. New York: National Bureau of Economic Research, distributed by Columbia University Press, 1976.

Mamalakis, Markos. *The Growth and Structure of the Chilean Economy: From Independence to Allende*. New Haven: Yale University Press, 1976.

Mamalakis, Markos, and Reynolds, Clark. *Essays on the Chilean Economy*. Homewood, IL: Richard D. Irwin, 1965.

## Colombia

Berry, R. Albert, and Urrutia, Miguel. *Income Distribution in Colombia*. New Haven: Yale University Press, 1976.

Diaz Alejandro, Carlos F. *Colombia (Foreign Trade Regimes and Economic Development)*. New York: National Bureau of Economic Research, distributed by Columbia University Press, 1976.

International Labour Organisation, *Towards Full Employment: A Programme for Colombia*. Prepared by an interagency team organized by the International Labour Office, Geneva: 1970.

McGreevey, William Paul. *An Economic History of Colombia, 1845–1930*. London and New York: Cambridge University Press, 1971.

Nelson, Richard; Schultz, T. Paul; and Slighton, Richard L. *Structural Change in a Developing Economy*. Princeton: Princeton University Press, 1971.

## Cuba

Dominguez, Jorge J. *Cuba: Order and Revolution*. Cambridge: Harvard University Press, 1978.

Mesa-Largo, Carmelo. *The Economy of Socialist Cuba: A Two-Decade Appraisal*. Albuquerque: University of New Mexico Press, 1981.

Wallich, Henry C. *Monetary Problems of an Export Economy: The Cuban Experience, 1914–1947*. Cambridge: Harvard University Press, 1950.

## Mexico

Hansen, Roger D. *The Politics of Mexican Development*. Baltimore: Johns Hopkins University Press, 1971.

Reynolds, Clark W. *The Mexican Economy: Twentieth Century Structure and Growth*. New Haven: Yale University Press, 1970.

Singer, Morris. *Growth, Equality and the Mexican Experience*. Austin: the University of Texas Press for the Institute of Latin American Studies, 1969.

## Peru

Thorp, Rosemary, and Bertram, Geoffrey. *Peru, 1890–1977: Growth and Policy in an Open Economy*. New York: Columbia University Press, 1978.

## Venezuela

Brito Figueroa, Federico. *História Económica y Social de Venezuela: Una Estructura para su Estudio*. Caracas: Dirección de Cultura, Universidad Central de Venezuela, 1966.

Martz, J., and Myers, D., eds. *Venezuela: The Democratic Experience*. New York: Praeger, 1977.

Tugwell, Franklin. *The Politics of Oil in Venezuela*. Stanford: Stanford University Press, 1975.

### NORTH AFRICA AND THE MIDDLE EAST

### General

Amin, Samir. *The Maghreb in the Modern World: Algeria, Tunisia, Morocco*. Harmondsworth: Penguin, 1970.

Issawi, Charles. *The Economic History of the Middle East, 1800–1914*. Chicago: University of Chicago Press, 1966.

———. *An Economic History of the Middle East and North Africa*. New York: Columbia University Press, 1982.

Sa'igh, Yusif A. *The Economies of the Arab World: Development since 1945*. New York: St. Martin's Press, 1978.

### Egypt

Abdel-Fadil, Mahmoud. *Development, Income Distribution and Social Change in Rural Egypt, 1952–1970: A Study in the Political Economy of Agrarian Transition*. Cambridge and New York: Cambridge University Press, 1975.

Hansen, Bent, and Marzouk, G. A. *Development and Economic Policy in the UAR*. Amsterdam: North-Holland, 1965.

Hansen, Bent, and Nashashibi, Karim. *Egypt (Foreign Trade Regimes and Economic Development)*. New York: National Bureau of Economic Research, distributed by Columbia University Press, 1975.

Mabro, Robert. *The Egyptian Economy, 1952–1972*. Oxford: Clarendon Press, 1974.

Mead, Donald C. *Growth and Structural Change in the Egyptian Economy*. Homewood, IL: Richard D. Irwin, 1967.

### Iran

Amuzegar, Jahangin, and Fekrat, W. Ali. *Iran: Economic Development under Dualistic Conditions*. Chicago: University of Chicago Press, 1971.

Bharier, Julian. *Economic Development in Iran, 1900–1970*. London and New York: Oxford University Press, 1971.

Issawi, Charles, ed. *The Economic History of Iran, 1800–1914*. Chicago: University of Chicago Press, 1971.

## Iraq

Penrose, Edith, and Penrose, E. F. *Iraq: International Relations and National Development*. Boulder, CO: Westview Press, 1978.

## Morocco

Steward, Charles F. *The Economy of Morocco, 1912–1962*. Cambridge: Harvard University Press, 1964.

## Turkey

Hershlag, Z. Y. *Turkey: An Economy in Transition*. The Hague: Van Keulen, 1958.

Krueger, Anne O. *Turkey (Foreign Trade Regimes and Economic Development)*. New York: National Bureau of Economic Research, distributed by Columbia University Press, 1974.

Thornburg, M. W., et al. *Turkey: An Economic Appraisal*. New York: Twentieth Century Fund, 1949.

## SUB-SAHARAN AFRICA

## General

Anthony, K. R. M.; Johnston, Bruce F.; Jones, William O.; and Uchenda, Victor C. *Agricultural Change in Tropical Africa*. Ithaca: Cornell University Press, 1979.

Duffy, James. *Portuguese Africa*. Cambridge: Harvard University Press, 1959.

Duignan, Peter, and Gann, L. H., eds. *Colonialism in Africa, 1870–1960*. 2 vols. London and New York: Cambridge University Press, 1969, 1970.

Fieldhouse, Daniel K. "The Economic Exploitation of Africa: Some British and French Comparisons." In *France and Britain in Africa: Imperial Rivalry and Colonial Rule,* ed. Prosser Gifford and W. Roger Louis, pp. 593–662. New Haven: Yale University Press, 1971.

Hopkins, Anthony G. *An Economic History of West Africa*. New York: Columbia University Press, 1973.

International Bank for Reconstruction and Development. *Accelerated Development in Sub-Saharan Africa*. Washington, DC: IBRD, 1981.

Munro, J. Forbes. *Africa and the International Economy, 1800–1960*. Totowa, NJ: Rowman and Littlefield, 1976.

Robson, P., and Lury, D. A., eds. *The Economies of Africa*. London: Allen and
Unwin, 1969.

## Ghana

Leith, J. Clark. *Ghana (Foreign Trade Regimes and Economic Development)*.
New York: National Bureau of Economic Research, distributed by Columbia
University Press, 1974.

## Ivory Coast

Suret-Canale, Jean. *French Colonialism in Tropical Africa, 1900–1945*. London:
C. Hurst, 1971.
den Tuinder, Bastian, ed. *Ivory Coast: The Challenge of Success*. Baltimore:
Johns Hopkins University Press for the World Bank, 1978.

## Kenya

Hazelwood, Arthur. *The Economy of Kenya*. Oxford and New York: Oxford
University Press, 1979.
Van Zwanenberg, R. M. A., and King, Anne. *An Economic History of Kenya and
Uganda, 1800–1970*. London and New York: Macmillan, 1975.
Wolff, Richard D. *The Economics of Colonialism: Britain and Kenya, 1870–
1930*. New Haven: Yale University Press, 1974.

## Mozambique

United States Department of Agriculture. *Mozambiqués Agricultural Economy in
Brief*. Foreign Agricultural Economics Report no. 116. Washington, DC:
USDA, 1976.

## Nigeria

Ekundare, R. Olufemi. *An Economic History of Nigeria, 1860–1960*. New York:
Africana, 1973.
Helleiner, Gerald. *Peasant Agriculture, Government, and Economic Growth in
Nigeria*. Homewood, IL: Richard D. Irwin, 1966.
Kilby, Peter. *Industrialization in an Open Economy: Nigeria, 1945–1966*. New
York: Cambridge University Press, 1967.

## Tanzania

Clark, W. Edmund. *Socialist Development and Public Investment in Tanzania,
1964–73*. Toronto and Buffalo: University of Toronto Press, 1978.

Coulson, Andrew. *Tanzania, 1800–1980: A Political Economy.* New York: Oxford University Press, 1982.

Sabot, R. N. *Economic Development and Urban Migration: Tanzania, 1900–1971.* New York: Oxford University Press, 1979.

Stephens, Hugh W. *The Political Transformation of Tanganyika, 1920–1967.* New York: Praeger, 1968.

## Zaire

Anstey, Roger. *King Leopold's Legacy: The Congo under Belgian Rule, 1908–1960.* London and New York: Oxford University Press, 1966.

*Facts about the Congo Economy.* Brussels: Belgian Congo Information and Public Relations Office, 1960.

Grau, Guy, ed. *Zaire: The Political Economy of Underdevelopment.* New York: Praeger, 1979.

## Zambia

Baldwin, Robert E. *Economic Development and Export Growth: Northern Rhodesia, 1920–1960.* Berkeley: University of California Press, 1966.

Beveridge, Andrew A., and Oberschall, Anthony R. *African Businessmen and Development in Zambia.* Princeton: Princeton University Press, 1979.

Deane, Phyllis. *Colonial Social Accounting.* Cambridge: Cambridge University Press, 1953.

Dodge, Doris Jansen. *Agricultural Policy and Performance in Zambia: History, Prospects and Proposals for Change.* Berkeley: Institute of International Studies, University of California, 1977.

Obidegwy, C. F., and Nziramasanga, M. *Copper and Zambia.* Lexington: Lexington Books, 1981.

## Zimbabwe

Barber, William J. *The Economy of British Central Africa: A Case Study of Economic Development in a Dualistic Society.* Stanford: Stanford University Press, 1961.

Zimbabwe. "Towards a New Order—An Economic and Social Survey." Working Papers. New York: United Nations, Economic and Social Council, 1980.

# Index

# Economic Growth Center Book Publications

Werner Baer, *Industrialization and Economic Development in Brazil* (1965). Out of print.

Werner Baer and Isaac Kerstenetzky, eds., *Inflation and Growth in Latin America* (1964). Out of print.

Bela A. Balassa, *Trade Prospects for Developing Countries* (1964). Out of print.

Albert Berry and Miguel Urrutia, *Income Distribution in Colombia* (1976).

Hans P. Binswanger and Mark R. Rosenzweig, eds., *Contractual Arrangements, Employment, and Wages in Rural Labor Markets in Asia* (1983).

Thomas B. Birnberg and Stephen A. Resnick, *Colonial Development: An Econometric Study* (1975).

Benjamin I. Cohen, *Multinational Firms and Asian Exports* (1975).

Carlos F. Díaz Alejandro, *Essays on the Economic History of the Argentine Republic* (1970).

Robert Evenson and Yoav Kislev, *Agricultural Research and Productivity* (1975).

John C. H. Fei and Gustav Ranis, *Development of Labor Surplus Economy: Theory and Policy* (1964). Out of print.

Gerald K. Helleiner, *Peasant Agriculture, Government, and Economic Growth in Nigeria* (1966). Out of print.

Samuel P. S. Ho, *Economic Development of Taiwan, 1860–1970* (1978).

Nurul Islam, *Foreign Trade and Economic Controls in Development: The Case of United Pakistan* (1981).

Lawrence R. Klein and Kazushi Ohkawa, eds., *Economic Growth: The Japanese Experience since the Meiji Era* (1968). Out of print.

Paul W. Kuznets, *Economic Growth and Structure in the Republic of Korea* (1977).

A. Lamfalussy, *The United Kingdom and the Six* (1963). Out of print.

Markos J. Mamalakis, *The Growth and Structure of the Chilean Economy: From Independence to Allende* (1976). Out of print.

Markos J. Mamalakis and Clark W. Reynolds, *Essays on the Chilean Economy* (1965). Out of print.

Donald C. Mead, *Growth and Structural Change in the Egyptian Economy* (1967). Out of print.

Richard Moorsteen and Raymond P. Powell, *The Soviet Capital Stock* (1966). Out of print.

Kazushi Ohkawa and Miyohei Shinohara, eds. (with Larry Meissner), *Patterns of Japanese Economic Development: A Quantitative Appraisal* (1979).

Douglas S. Paauw and John C. H. Fei, *The Transition in Open Dualistic Economies: Theory and Southeast Asian Experience* (1973).

Howard Pack, *Structural Change and Economic Policy in Israel* (1971).

Frederick L. Pryor, *Public Expenditures in Communist and Capitalist Nations* (1968). Out of print.

Gustav Ranis, ed., *Government and Economic Development* (1971).

Clark W. Reynolds, *The Mexican Economy: Twentieth-Century Structure and Growth* (1970). Out of print.

Lloyd G. Reynolds, *Economic Growth in the Third World, 1850–1980* (1985).

Lloyd G. Reynolds, *Image and Reality in Economic Development* (1977).

Lloyd G. Reynolds, ed., *Agriculture in Development Theory* (1975).

Lloyd G. Reynolds and Peter Gregory, *Wages, Productivity, and Industrialization in Puerto Rico* (1965). Out of print.

Donald R. Snodgrass, *Ceylon: An Export Economy in Transition* (1966). Out of print.